RAND

Designing New American Schools

Baseline Observations on Nine Design Teams

*Susan Bodilly, Susanna Purnell,
Kimberly Ramsey, Christina Smith*

*Supported by the
New American Schools Development Corporation*

**Institute on Education
and Training**

This report is an analytic description of the initial efforts of the New American Schools Development Corporation (NASDC), a private nonprofit corporation created as part of the America 2000 initiative to fund the development of new designs for American schools. Between July 1993 and June 1995, NASDC funded nine teams to develop and demonstrate designs for high-performing schools.

NASDC asked RAND to be the analytical arm of its efforts at school reform. In particular, it gave RAND four tasks:

- Analyze the experiences of the design teams as they develop and demonstrate their designs in real schools and distill lessons for both future implementers of these designs and future designers of new designs.

- Monitor and ultimately synthesize the design teams' efforts to provide evidence of the initial effect of each design.

- Assess the costs of implementing each design for potential adopters.

- Identify systemic barriers to the scale-up of NASDC-supported designs.

This report describes the initial NASDC efforts and compares and contrasts the nine different designs and their demonstration strategies. The descriptions represent a baseline for the design teams' efforts.

This report and subsequent ones on the NASDC experience should interest educational policymakers at all levels of government, school administrators and teachers, and communities concerned with improved schooling.

The research was supported by NASDC. The study was conducted under the auspices of the Institute on Education and Training of the Domestic Research Division of RAND.

CONTENTS

FIGURES

TABLES

The New American Schools Development Corporation (NASDC) was established to develop "break the mold" schools that serve all students well and that do not cost substantially more to operate in the long run than other schools do. NASDC is using its funding to support several teams as they develop designs for high-performing schools and demonstrate design concepts through implementation in real schools. In 1991, NASDC solicited designs for such schools from independent groups through a request-for-proposal (RFP) process. Eleven teams, later reduced to nine teams, were chosen to both develop and demonstrate their concepts in real schools over a three-year time span, from July 1992 through June 1995. These are:

- Audrey Cohen College System of Education (AC).

- Authentic Teaching, Learning, and Assessment for All Students (AT).

- Community Learning Centers (CLC).

- Co-NECT (CON).

- Expeditionary Learning (EL).

- Los Angeles Learning Center (LALC).

- Modern Red Schoolhouse (MRSH).

- National Alliance for Restructuring Education (NA).

- Roots and Wings (RW).

The teams were given one year (called Phase 1) from mid-year 1992 to mid-year 1993, to consolidate their teams and further develop the concepts of their designs from the visions described in their proposals. In Phase 2, the teams were given two years, ending in June 1995, to further develop and demonstrate their designs in real schools. In Phase 3, the teams are expected to enter a new group of schools and provide more adept assistance based upon lessons learned and materials developed in Phase 2.

PURPOSE

NASDC asked RAND to study the efforts of the nine design teams and their respective sites to inform the public about the contributions of design teams to reform and to identify barriers to the change process in schools. This report, the first in a series, provides baseline information about the designs to understand how the designs might subsequently develop and evolve from concepts to demonstrations in real schools. This report addresses several questions:

- What are the principal elements of the designs and how do the designs compare and contrast on these elements?

- What approaches are being used to develop the designs?

- What factors might affect the teams' ability to demonstrate their designs in Phase 2?

- What are the implications of these differences for Phase 2 and Phase 3?

METHOD

The research uses a comparative case study approach with the design team as the unit of analysis and the nine designs compared and contrasted. Two sites were chosen for each team to form an embedded case study that includes the team, the district, the schools, and individuals associated with the schools. The research team reviewed all proposals, design documents, and interim reports submitted to NASDC by the design teams. In fall 1993, teams of two staff members visited each design team and two sites. Interviews were conducted with district officials, school principals, key design-related site personnel, teachers, and, when possible, parents and business partners.

DESIGN AND DESIGN TEAM COMPARISONS

The designs and teams differed in many details, but we found, at a macro level, four fundamental differences among teams: the scope of the design and needed collaborators, the development and demonstration strategy chosen, the readiness of the team for Phase 2, and the selection of sites.

Design Characteristics

Designs differed in their breadth of coverage and needed collaboration. Three approaches distinguish the designs.

Core designs (AC, CON, EL, and RW) emphasize changes in seven elements associated with the core of schooling: curriculum, instruction, standards, assessments, student groupings, community involvement, and professional development. They focus on school-level partnerships—it is their main point of entry and continued interaction.

Comprehensive designs (AT, CLC, LALC, and MRSH) emphasize more elements, including integrated social services, governance changes, and organization and staffing changes as fundamental to the design. These latter elements are intended to indirectly affect the schools over time. Although these teams believe that they need to construct complex collaborative efforts with groups outside of schools to accomplish these goals, their main interventions are still at the school-building level.

The sole **systemic** design (NA) emphasizes changes to all elements and the need for collaboration among many partners. Rather than focusing on the school as the intervention point, this design focuses on changing the systems that surround schools including the central office, state legislation, professional development providers, social services providers, and the community.

Development Approaches

The teams clustered into three groups in terms of who would be responsible for further specifying and developing the designs. Specification refers to deciding what elements belong in a design and the general nature of those elements. Development refers to the creation of materials, lesson plans, models, and resources that fill out the design and will be used to transfer the ideas of the design to new sites in Phase 3.

Team Specified and Developed: One group of teams, including AC and RW, relies more heavily than others on the capabilities of the design team to further specify and develop the design. These teams take responsibility for specifying standards, curriculum frameworks, models of lesson plans, lists of resources, models for student assignment, and assessments in keeping with the design.

Locally Specified and Developed: In contrast, another set of teams (AT, CLC, and NA) provides guidelines and resources to schools for a process of change by which the schools specify and develop their own designs in keeping with principles of the design team. The schools specify what they will become and develop their own curriculum, choose what kind of student groupings are appropriate, etc.

Design Team Specified and Locally Developed: A final group of teams (CON, EL, LALC, and MRSH) takes major responsibility in specifying the design, but will rely on the sites to further develop the models, curriculum, assessments, assignments, etc.

Readiness Factors

The design teams also appear to differ in terms of their existing team capability. They vary as to whether the team was newly created, whether it needed to put in place a staff and structure to undertake the effort, whether the leadership of the team had to develop or be transferred, and whether the team or team members as a group lacked experience in implementation of school-level reform.

Two teams (AC and RW) began with existing organizations with strong school reform experience. There was no transfer between those who wrote the proposal and the team that would execute it. Three other teams (CLC, CON, and NA) had some prior experience or organizational base, but were handicapped in other ways. Four teams (AT, EL, LALC, and MRSH) faced Phase 2 with significantly greater challenges than the other teams regarding their readiness, because they had to assemble new teams and organizations.

Site Choices

For the most part, no pattern of site selection emerged across design teams. The selection process appeared idiosyncratic and driven more by NASDC deadlines than by a thoughtful process. The teams did choose different numbers of schools, with CON and LALC working with only two schools each and NA working in over 80 schools across many districts.

IMPLICATIONS FOR PHASE 2

NASDC set out to develop the capability of a diverse set of teams and designs to effect school reform. Our descriptions in this document indicate that it has accomplished part of this goal. We draw two simple conclusions. First, NASDC selected and promoted through Phase 1 a diverse set of designs that included different approaches to reform as well as different strategies for how to demonstrate reforms in the Phase 2 period. Second, the diversity of the design teams and designs should lead to different expectations for Phase 2 performance.

Those teams with core designs, a team specification and development approach, strong indications of readiness, and a modest number of sites are more likely to emerge from Phase 2 with well-developed designs and potentially with strong demonstration sites. Two teams fit this description: AC and RW.

Teams with three or more of the following will likely show slower progress and this progress will vary significantly from school to school: comprehensive or systemic designs (designs that cover more elements including governance changes, integrated social services, and staffing changes), local specification and development, challenges in terms of readiness, and concentration in a few schools or in many schools. Three teams fit this description: AT, LALC, and NA.

A group of teams falls somewhere between these two extremes, having some challenges (CON, EL, MRSH, and CLC). All required significant local development approaches. Two (MRSH and CLC) include many elements in the design. Three (CON, EL, and MRSH) had challenges related to team readiness. Finally, CON is focusing all its efforts in a few sites.

IMPLICATIONS FOR PHASE 3

In Phase 3, NASDC will enter into agreements with a limited number of interested districts to transform schools in those districts using the design teams as assistance organizations. The Phase 3 strategy for NASDC offers districts and schools choices among assistance organizations and their designs. Given the nature of the teams and the demonstrations in Phase 2, we think that the designs will vary in their ability to demonstrate a coherent picture of their particular reform to potential Phase 3 adopters. NASDC and the teams must find ways to help potential adopters understand and interpret the important differences among them and set expectations for improvement and required resources accordingly.

ACKNOWLEDGMENTS

We would like to thank the New American Schools Development Corporation (NASDC) for its support for studying the implementation efforts of the nine design teams and of NASDC in general. This study would not have been possible without the aid and cooperation of the design teams, districts, and sites involved in the NASDC effort. People in each organization gave freely of their time to enable us to understand the issues involved in developing and demonstrating new designs for schools. We thank them for their efforts regarding this study, and also for their dedication to improving the educational prospects of all children.

AC	Audrey Cohen College System of Education
ACT	AT Communities Team
AT	Authentic Teaching, Learning, and Assessment of All Students
CEO	Chief Educational Officer
CLC	Community Learning Centers
CON	Co-NECT
CRESST	Center for Research and Evaluation, Standards and Student Testing
CSTEEP	Center for the Study of Testing, Evaluation, and Educational Policy
EL	Expeditionary Learning
LAEP	Los Angeles Educational Partnership
LALC	Los Angeles Learning Center
LAUSD	Los Angeles Unified School District
MRSH	Modern Red Schoolhouse
NA	National Alliance for Restructuring Education
NASDC	New American Schools Development Corporation
NCTM	The National Council of Teachers of Mathematics
NSP	New Standards Project
PLP	Personal Learning Plan
RFP	Request for Proposal
RW	Roots and Wings
SPMT	School Planning and Management Team
UTLA	United Teachers of Los Angeles

Chapter One

INTRODUCTION

In July 1991, the New American Schools Development Corporation (NASDC) was established to develop designs and design teams capable of transforming current schools into high-performing schools that prepare all students well. Funded largely by the private sector, it began a unique development program. It sought to engage the nation's best educators, business people, and researchers in the creation of teams that would develop and demonstrate whole-school designs. The idea was to contribute to the national effort to improve schools by creating the capability in several teams to provide designs and school-level assistance that could more quickly and reliably aid whole-school transformation.

A year later, following a major national competition, NASDC announced it was awarding contracts to 11 teams for a year-long design effort. In July 1993, nine teams were awarded two-year contracts to demonstrate their designs in two or more schools in what NASDC termed its Phase 2 development effort. Currently, the nine design teams are developing and refining their concepts in 147 schools in 19 states. Judging by early indications of successful practice, seven teams will become part of a national scale-up effort designed to foster the implementation of their designs in many schools across the country.

PURPOSE OF THIS REPORT

Because it is simultaneously funding nine designs, the NASDC program provides a unique opportunity to identify both common and distinctive features of designs and approaches to whole-school reform. To the extent that NASDC school designs represent a reasonable vision of what schools should be in the future, this analysis suggests something of the state- and district-level reforms that will be needed if designs such as these are to become widespread.

The principal purpose of this report is to develop a conceptual framework for comparing the NASDC designs. It provides, in a limited sense, the means for measuring the evolution of designs, as it reports on the designs at an early stage in their development. This report answers four questions:

- What are the principal elements of the designs and how do the designs compare and contrast on these elements?

- What approaches are being used to develop the designs?

- What factors might affect the teams' ability to demonstrate their designs?

- What are the implications of these differences for Phase 2 and Phase 3?

The observations in this report are based upon field work and document reviews from fall 1993. Future reports will provide more information on demonstration experiences and changes to designs in light of barriers.

METHOD

The research uses a comparative case study approach with the design team as the unit of analysis and the nine designs compared and contrasted. Two sites were chosen for each team to form an embedded case study that includes the team, the district, the schools, and individuals associated with the schools. The data collected and reviewed includes

- Background materials such as school reports, district data on conditions in the schools, newspaper reports, etc.

- Documents produced by NASDC, the teams, and schools describing their purposes and efforts.

- Interviews with important actors including design team members, parents in governing committees, lead or master teachers, site coordinators and facilitators, school administrators, district administrators, and state administrators.

- Group interviews of teachers and parents.

- Observation of school activities and a limited number of classes.

The research team reviewed all proposals, design documents, and interim reports submitted to NASDC by the design teams. Staff members also made at least one visit to each of the teams during the design phase of the projects. In summer 1993, RAND staff attended the various summer institutes and staff development meetings held by all the design teams except one. In fall 1993, teams of two staff members visited each design team and at least two sites where each team's design was being implemented. Interviews were conducted with district officials, school principals, key design-related site personnel, teachers, and, when possible, parents and business partners.

ORGANIZATION OF THE REPORT

The remainder of the report is organized as follows. Chapter Two describes the purposes of NASDC and provides a brief history to date. Chapter Three describes the approach that RAND has taken to tracking and analyzing the development of the designs. Chapter Four provides general contrasts between the designs in terms of their breadth. Chapter Five discusses development strategies of the teams. Chapter Six discusses the readiness of the teams for the tasks they are undertaking. Chapter Seven describes local site issues and how they might affect the teams. Chapter Eight summarizes the implication of the above chapters for expectations of progress during Phase 2 and points to some implications for Phase 3.

Appendix A provides a synopsis of each of the designs, following the element list used in the body of this report. Appendix B describes the sites that are implementing the designs during the 1993–1995 school years.

Chapter Two

NASDC's PURPOSE AND HISTORY

We begin with a short review of the NASDC mission and key events that have shaped its program. This will provide the context for understanding the purpose of NASDC and the challenges faced by the teams.

FORMATION OF THE CORPORATION

NASDC was a prominent part of President George Bush's America 2000 educational initiative announced by Education Secretary Lamar Alexander in April 1991. The proposal followed the agreement on a set of national goals for education between the President and the National Governors Association, a forum presided over by then Governor Bill Clinton. Among other things, America 2000 proposed the development of voluntary national standards in major subject areas, called for the creation of America 2000 communities that would marshal resources to support the development of high-performance schools, and proposed that $535 million be allocated for the creation of break-the-mold schools. NASDC, with private sector funding, was to promote teams to create designs and implementation supports that might be used by the New American Schools but would be made widely available to all.

David Kearns, the Deputy Secretary of Education, played an important role in creating NASDC itself. He recruited a prestigious board made up largely of chief executive officers of major American corporations. Some $40 million was immediately pledged to support NASDC, a nonprofit corporation. The informal working group that helped to organize the corporation set a larger goal of $150 million to

$200 million over a projected five-year lifetime. The initial NASDC literature suggested that five to seven teams made up of businesses, think tanks, universities, and educators would be supported to develop designs that were to set aside the existing conventions and rules governing the design of schools.

Formation of the corporation was announced in a Rose Garden ceremony at the White House in July 1991. The first president of NASDC was Frank Blount, an executive on loan from AT&T.

PURPOSES OF NASDC AND KEY CONCEPTS

NASDC is unique in education reform efforts because of the purposefulness with which it has undertaken the development of the capability to transform schools.

Goals

Over the past decade, a school reform intervention has been slowly emerging that involves the creation of design and assistance organizations, peopled by experts with a common vision and goal who offer assistance to individual schools interested in transforming themselves. Examples of such organizations include the Coalition for Essential Schools, the Accelerated Schools, Paidaeia, Success For All, and the School Development Program of Yale's Child Study Center. Individually they have different emphases and different intervention strategies. In common they exhibit the same approach—a team of outside experts assisting individual schools. Each has had some compelling successes. Each also grew slowly because of lack of sustained resources for development. They often grew by fits and starts in a serendipitous fashion out of small research efforts. As Robert Slavin, head of Success For All, said, "we always have had money for research and evaluation of school programs, but never for development of successful intervention programs."[1]

---

[1]Interview by RAND staff with Robert Slavin, October 14, 1993, Johns Hopkins University.

NASDC is an extensive and formalized effort to provide resources for the systematic development of teams and their designs, including implementation supports, and to support these teams' efforts as they aid real schools in their transformation. Its purpose is to, in a five-year period:

- Develop a diverse group of design teams capable of leading schools through the transformation process.

- Sustain the teams in the development of diverse but clear designs that can be used by others.

- Provide observable demonstration and testing of the designs, along with evidence that improved schools can be sustained in diverse jurisdictions.

- Create a well-documented history of the findings, lessons learned, successes, and failures of the NASDC enterprise.

Phases

From the beginning, those who supported the NASDC effort have been dedicated to observable results within a five-year time frame. The five-year period was divided into four phases as shown in Figure 2.1.

Pre-Phase 1: The first few months would be dedicated to a competitive request-for-proposal (RFP) process for the selection of teams to be funded, based on a 50-page description of each potential design that included a vision statement, a development strategy, an assessment plan, a staffing plan, and a scale-up strategy for Phase 3.

Phase 1: The teams would then be given one year to further specify the designs and develop more detailed concepts as well as build the capability to demonstrate the designs in real sites.

Phase 2: The teams would then have two years to develop demonstration sites, while further developing the designs and implementation strategies based on feedback from real schools. The goal of Phase 2 is to have each team show that its design concepts can be

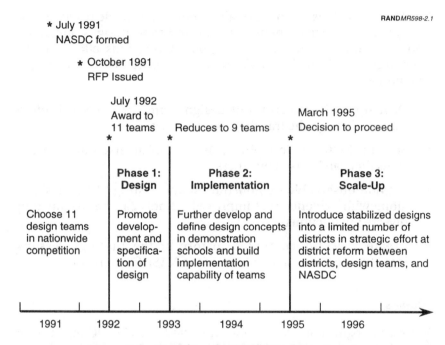

RAND*MR598-2.1*

Figure 2.1—Time Line for NASDC Reform Agenda

implemented in real schools and to develop demonstration sites by June 1995 to prove this and to act as a base for Phase 3 efforts.[2]

Phase 3: The design teams would help many schools to adapt and use their designs over another two-year period, while promoting further progress at the demonstration sites of Phase 2.

Phase 3 is a key part of the NASDC mission. Its founders were anxious not to simply create a few high-quality model schools. The RFP stated,

> *This is not a request to establish "model" schools.* NASDC does not seek to develop "cookie cutter" designs. The designs must be adaptable so that they can be used by many communities to create

---

[2]Some who founded NASDC thought that all development would be completed by the end of Phase 1. However, the design teams continue to develop through Phase 2.

their own new schools. A design team must have an effective plan to generate the energy required for local communities to create their own high-performance, break-the-mold schools. The important thing is that long after NASDC has disappeared from the scene, its legacy of new designs will remain.[3]

PRE-PHASE 1: RFP PROCESS AND SELECTION OF TEAMS

The RFPs called for proposals for a five-year program in which bidders were invited to imagine a new kind of American school— public or private—in which:

- Assumptions about how students learn and what students should know and be able to do are completely reexamined;

- Visions of the nature and locations of schools are reconsidered; and

- The manner in which communities create, govern, and hold their schools accountable is redesigned.[4]

One criterion by which proposals were judged was their "potential for widespread application and the quality of plans for fostering such application."[5] The program possesses a strong business-oriented perspective: develop and test a new product and then go sell it.

The time schedule is short. It is common wisdom that school restructuring efforts take five years or longer. At a workshop held in July 1991 to help design the RFP, representatives of then existing design teams seemed to generally agree that it takes longer than five years. However, the NASDC board was unwilling to accept this answer. It believed that ambitious deadlines were required to deal with what they perceived as a critical national problem. Although the design teams could not create and fully prove designs in three years, sufficient progress and evidence would exist to permit other schools

---

[3]New American Schools Development Corporation (NASDC) (1991), p. 21, italics in original.

[4]NASDC (1991), p. 9.

[5]NASDC (1991), p. 35.

and school systems to decide whether the design held sufficient promise to merit adoption.

The RFP had several other important emphases as well.

- The designs were to integrate all elements of a school's life; they were to be for whole schools, not just a single grade or program within a school.

- They were to be "benchmarked" against demanding goals and achievement standards.

- The designs were to be for all students, not merely for those students most likely to succeed.[6]

Thus, NASDC decided that a school or a group of schools was the appropriate target of reform. NASDC was created by people who believed that there should be high standards coupled with appropriate means of assessing performance against those standards.

Finally, and perhaps most importantly for the designs themselves, the schools had to be able to help virtually all students to reach these standards. This would force the designers to choose curricular and instructional strategies that could accommodate the varied learning styles of the nation's youth.

Up to $20 million was to be potentially available to each team, allowing the development money that had not been provided to most reformers in the past.

Blount announced that he wanted a draft RFP ready for public review by the end of August 1991. Design conferences were held to explain the RFP in August and September and a final RFP was issued in mid-October 1991. Fifty-page proposals were due on February 14, 1992.

The response was overwhelming. As one of the ultimate winners put it, NASDC was the "only game in town." Nearly 700 proposals were received. To review the proposals, NASDC held three four-day selection sessions involving more than 500 people from education, business, universities, and professional organizations. The review

---

[6]NASDC (1991), pp. 20 and 21.

quickly narrowed the field down to approximately 30 proposals considered worth pursuing. Most proposals were easily dismissed on the grounds that they sought funding to implement interesting programs at a few schools, without offering schoolwide reform that could be adopted across sites. Following the review and that of NASDC's staff, NASDC announced it would make awards to 11 teams for the initial design effort.

Each of the 11 teams entered into negotiations with NASDC and NASDC awarded funding based on its judgment concerning the needs of the particular teams. The amount of funding pledged to teams varied substantially.

PHASE 1 AND FUNDING ISSUES

Although the solicitation and selection process moved along roughly on schedule, NASDC's fund-raising efforts stalled. Over the first twelve months, almost no additional funding was obtained and the continuation of the program became increasingly precarious. The initial pledges provided sufficient funds to support the Phase 1 effort, but plans for continuation were dependent on raising additional money. Plans for conferences and institutes intended to launch the designs had to be scaled back because of lack of funds and, in spring 1993, there were doubts whether adequate funding would be available for the demonstration of the designs.

A number of factors contributed to the fund-raising problems. Blount left for a new job in the telecommunications industry. His successor, former Secretary of Labor Ann McLaughlin, resigned after about 8 months because she felt she was unable to devote sufficient time to the job. Moreover, in the initial phase, the U.S. economy was in recession and many firms in the private sector were cutting back on their contributions.

In spring 1993, David Kearns became president and CEO of NASDC and initiated new efforts to seek funding.

PHASE 2 AND THE TEAMS

In May 1993, President Clinton and Secretary of Education Riley strongly endorsed NASDC as an activity that complemented the

Goals 2000 program that they had submitted to the Congress. With that endorsement, Kearns and members of the board succeeded in raising sufficient funding to initiate the demonstration of the designs in July 1993. In the fall, Ambassador Walter Annenberg announced that he was donating an additional $50 million to NASDC (he had already contributed $10 million), which would allow it to complete the Phase 2 demonstrations.

At the end of the first year of Phase 2, two of the 11 teams were judged to have failed to meet the objectives that were agreed upon and to lack promise for wide-scale implementation. Nine teams were chosen to go forward. These nine teams again entered into negotiations and NASDC again awarded funding that varied substantially by team. These nine teams are presently completing Phase 2. Seven teams have been selected, based on performance to date, to further develop their designs, build demonstration sites, and participate in Phase 3 national scale-up efforts.

Brief descriptions of the designs that did move forward follow. We note that the following statements encapsulate the visions of the designs, not the realities of their demonstration, which remain to be seen.

Audrey Cohen College System of Education (AC)

A holistic and purpose-driven curriculum is the centerpiece of the design. This interdisciplinary, applied learning curriculum focuses on the purposes of learning and leads students through a series of constructive social actions. All associated activities in the school change to support the learning purposes. For grades K–12.

Authentic Teaching, Learning, and Assessment of All Students (AT)

The design requires a participatory governance structure focused on a K-12 feeder pattern (pathway). Although it has strong principles of interdisciplinary curriculum and instruction, the unique focus is on the consensus-building governance needed to lead away from fragmented, bureaucratic learning environments to unified support for a community of learners. For grades K–12.

Community Learning Centers (CLC)

The design requires that schools have an "institutional bypass" from the current system of regulations that bind school-level improvement. The core of the school is individualized instruction with continuous assessment of student and school progress. The school becomes the community center for education, social, and health services. For grades K–12.

Co-NECT (CON)

School-based design teams tailor a generic design to meet local needs. With district and community support, the local design is implemented, and continuously refined, by teams of empowered, accountable teachers. Modern technology, featuring desktop Internet participation, supports a project-based curriculum and continuous assessment of school and student progress. For grades K–12.

Expeditionary Learning (EL)

Dedicated to complete development of students and teachers by extending the values of Outward Bound into schools, the curriculum and instruction move toward expeditions of learning intended to develop intellectual, physical, and civic sides of students. Teachers become guides and are provided continuous, innovative professional development. For grades K–12.

Los Angeles Learning Center (LALC)

A unique partnership of the district, teachers' union, universities, businesses, and community groups to overcome urban distress and jointly build a school of the future dedicated to individual support. Emphasis is placed on strong social support for students from school and community members. For grades K–12.

Modern Red Schoolhouse (MRSH)

The design blends elements of traditional education with new instructional methods to provide all students with a strong foundation in American culture as well as skills needed for future employment. For grades K–12.

National Alliance for Restructuring Education (NA)

An alliance of states, districts, schools, and expert organizations created to effect system change at all levels by promoting ambitious standards and accountability mechanisms. The design focuses on results-based governance with decentralized decisionmaking and the provision of strong professional support to teachers and schools. For grades K–12.

Roots and Wings (RW)

A relentless and organized approach to ensuring that all children will leave elementary schools with skills required for success. The design reallocates existing federal, state, and local resources into a system of curriculum, instruction, and family support designed to eliminate special education and low achievement. For grades K–6.

The capsule comments above do not do justice to the diversity and vision of the designs, but are intended to provide more than the title alone would. Appendix A of this report contains a more detailed description of key elements of each design.

Chapter Three

RAND'S PURPOSE AND APPROACH

This chapter describes the role of RAND in the NASDC effort and more specifically addresses the methodology used for what has become known as the demonstration/implementation analysis that this document sets up.

RAND's PURPOSE

There are two goals for RAND's program of analyses for NASDC.

1. The first is to help NASDC and its design teams successfully accomplish their goal of developing, demonstrating, and scaling-up their designs. This requires immediate and private feedback to this group that will not be found in published reports.

2. The second is to analyze and synthesize the experiences of the design teams and their demonstration sites to provide information to potential users of the designs and to policymakers who are shaping the education system within which the designs will be implemented. The audience for this information is public and includes school, district, and state administrators, education reformers, journalists, and design teams not under NASDC's umbrella.

These goals are supported by four tasks undertaken between 1993 and 1995.

- Analyze the experiences of the design teams as they develop and demonstrate their designs in real schools and distill lessons for

15

both future adopters of these designs and future designers of new designs.

- Monitor and ultimately synthesize the design teams' efforts to provide evidence of the initial effect of each design.

- Assess the costs of implementing each design for potential adopters.

- Identify barriers to the scale-up of NASDC-supported designs.

This report deals primarily with the first and last tasks. We state unequivocally that the tasks are not evaluations. RAND is not now evaluating such results of the designs in schools as changed student performances or changed school performances. It instead is focusing on the question of implementation central to the notion of later evaluation.

A large school reform literature dating back to the "Change Agent Study[1]" indicates that a major problem in school reform is not that the interventions do not have desired effects but that the interventions are never implemented as proposed so as to have the desired effects. Recognizing this, the purpose of Phase 2 is to develop designs and demonstration sites to the point where the interventions are in place, if not fully stable, and effects could be expected. The question to be addressed precedes the more formal evaluation: Did the teams actually put in place the interventions they proposed? Once this is established and time allowed for effects to occur, evaluations of the effects of the interventions can take place.

Design teams are responsible for their own evaluations during Phase 2. Given the short period of time—two years in which to have a measurable effect in a school, and the developmental changes expected in the designs—we imagine that these evaluations will not be compelling. On the other hand, evaluations of the Phase 3 efforts, when designs have stabilized and teams can implement them, would make more sense and are expected to show more compelling evidence for support or nonsupport of future design team efforts.

---

[1]Berman and McLaughlin (1975).

CASE STUDY APPROACH

The phenomenon to be studied is the model of change adopted by NASDC—the creation and intervention of an entity called a design team to promote school reform. The phenomenon includes the development of the teams as well as their experiences in demonstrating their designs. This highly complex process lends itself to case study analysis. The evidence sought is qualitative—actors' descriptions and assessments of their experiences and barriers to their desired actions. We rely entirely on the differences among the teams and their sites to provide the contrasts to be studied.

UNIT OF ANALYSIS AND CHOICE OF SITES

The design team and its design is considered the unit of analysis, resulting in nine cases. We expect the relationships of each design to its demonstration sites to be unique and to offer interesting insights. Therefore, the subunit of analysis will be the school or district (when appropriate as the design team's intervention point).

For each team we have chosen two schools or districts to study with agreement by the team and NASDC. For example, the CON design has chosen to work in two schools in two different districts. These two schools form the basis for observations about the ability of the team to demonstrate its design in real schools. However, the AT design's construct is a feeder pattern of schools (referred to in their design as a pathway) including the elementary schools, middle schools, and common high school that serve a geographic area. The unit of analysis for this team is the pathway consisting of several schools. Thus, for AT we chose two pathways to study and each pathway includes several schools.

The sample includes urban and rural schools and districts, elementary schools, middle schools, and high schools, poor schools, and not-so-poor schools. Table 3.1 shows some of the key features of the sample.

Table 3.1

Characteristics of the Sample Sites

Design Team	School	Grade Span	Enrollment	Free and Reduced-Price Lunch (%)	Setting
AC					
Phoenix, AZ[a]	Loma Linda	K–8	1200	90	Urban
San Diego, CA[b]	Alcott	K–5	395	40[a]	Urban
	Franklin	K–5	540	72	Urban
AT					
Gorham, ME[c,d]	Gorham High School	9–12	500	16[e]	Small city/rural
	Little Falls	K	200	16[e]	Small city/rural
	Narragansett	1–3	473	16[e]	Small city/rural
	Shaw	7–8	340	16[e]	Small city/rural
	Village	4–6	600	16[e]	Small city/rural
	White Rock	1–3	166	16[e]	Small city/rural
Prince George's County, MD	Adelphi[a]	PK–3	505	74	Urban
	Buck Lodge[f]	6–8	675	78	Urban
	Cool Spring[a]	PK–3	540	82	Urban
	High Point[f]	9–12	2117	40	Urban
	Langley Park[a]	4–6	515	92	Urban
CLC					
Cloquet, MN[g]	Fond du Lac	PK–12	231	n/a[h]	Reservation
Duluth, MN[d]	Spotted Eagle	K–6	106	n/a[h]	Small city
Minneapolis, MN[g]	Cedar-Riverside	K–6	82	90	Urban
CON					
Dorchester[i]	Sarah Greenwood	K–6+	348	98	Urban
Worcester, MA[g]	ALL School	K–8	466	80	Urban
EL					
Dubuque, IA	Bryant[g]	K–5	349	26[e]	Small city
	Lincoln[g]	K–5	419	26[e]	Small city
	Central	9–12	162	26[e]	Small city
New York, NY[a]	School for the Physical City	6–8,10	144	38	Urban

Table 3.1 (Continued)

Design Team	School	Grade Span	Enrollment	Free and Reduced-Price Lunch (%)	Setting
LALC					
Cudahy, CA[a]	Elizabeth Street	PK–10	2400	88	Urban
Los Angeles, CA[a]	Foshay	K–10	2700	89	Urban
MRSH					
Bartholomew, IN	Columbus East[a]	9–12	1234	8	Small city/rural
	Northside[a]	6–8	805	15	Small city/rural
	Taylorsville[f]	K–6	504	23	Small city/rural
Indianapolis, IN[f]	Frost	K–5	293	60	Urban
NA					
Louisville, KY[a]	Kennedy	K–5	411	66	Urban
Calloway County, KY[g]	Calloway Middle	6–8	727	38[j]	Rural
	Southwest Calloway	K–5	482	37[j]	Rural
San Diego, CA	Darnall[f]	K–5	407	90	Urban
	Marshall[g]	K–5	903	93	Urban
RW					
St. Mary's County, MD[c]	Ridge	PK–5	276	29	Rural
	Lexington Park	PK–5	474	42	Small city

[a]Data approximate as of spring 1995.
[b]Data reported in 1994.
[c]Data reported in 1991.
[d]Grade spans and enrollment as of 1993–1994 site visits.
[e]District-level data, not reported by individual school.
[f]Data reported in 1992.
[g]Data reported in 1993.
[h]These schools operate under the Bureau of Indian Affairs, and meals are provided in a different manner.
[i]The design team ended its relationship with this site during the school year 1993–1994.
[j]Percentage reported as "low-income."

DATA SOURCES AND TIMING

Because the designs are intended to influence people at many levels, as will be shown in the following chapters, an embedded case study is appropriate. We use many sources for information and many types of information:

- Background materials such as school reports, district data on conditions in the schools, newspaper reports, etc.

- Documents produced by NASDC, the teams, and schools describing their purposes and efforts.

- Interviews with important actors including design team members, parents in governing committees, lead or master teachers, site coordinators and facilitators, school administrators, district administrators, and state administrators.

- Group interviews of students, teachers, and parents.[2]

- Observation of school activities and a limited number of classes.

This information has been gathered in three waves: fall 1993 site visits, spring 1994 site visits, and spring 1995 site visits. Each site and team was visited three times during Phase 2. The last visit corresponds to the end of Phase 2. In addition, RAND staff has attended summer workshops held by teams and conferences when appropriate.

DATABASE FOR THIS REPORT

The description of designs and development plans reported in this document represent a baseline upon which to track the evolution of the designs during Phase 2. RAND staff has read and analyzed the

---

[2]The designs intend to affect all teachers and all students at the school level. To reach as many of these actors as possible, we chose to use group interview techniques. Group interview protocols were developed to elicit group views on issues involved in implementation and progress toward design team goals. This technique's strength is that it provides in-depth coverage of issues and personal experiences and allows for adaptation to the circumstances of particular designs and sites. However, its weakness is that it does not provide the statistical data of a survey. A survey instrument, however, could not elicit the depth of exploration required or be modified for over 30 different schools.

proposals, design documents produced at the end of Phase 1, and many of the interim reports that have been provided to NASDC by the teams. Staff made at least one visit to each of the teams during Phase 1. In summer 1993, staff attended parts of the summer institutes or staff development meetings that were held by all the teams but one. These visits allowed us to become familiar with the manner in which the design teams described their designs to their demonstration sites and the broad strategies they planned to use to further develop and demonstrate their designs.

In October, November, and December 1993 (Year 1, Phase 2), RAND teams, each consisting of two staff members, visited each design team and at least two sites at which the design was being implemented for each team. In addition to the design team staffs, interviews were normally conducted with the schools' principals, with key design-related site personnel such as facilitators and coordinators, and with a number of teachers. We also interviewed central office personnel and, in some instances, the superintendent. In some cases we talked with parents and volunteers. Each of these interviews was based on an interview protocol that was developed during summer 1993. Typically, we devoted about three person-days to each site. We visited 35 schools. This report is based on these interviews and the document review.

FUTURE DATA COLLECTIONS AND REPORTS

To complete the analysis, RAND visited the same 35 schools in spring 1994 and spring 1995, using a revised protocol.[3] The goal is to learn how the development and demonstration has evolved since its formative stages. We focused more explicitly on systemic barriers to the development and demonstration of the designs and on the real costs of implementing the designs. We sought to spend more time with teachers, parents, and governance teams. After review of the data gathered during visits in spring 1995, a final report will be disseminated.

---

[3]At the publishing of this report those visits have been made. This report is informed by those visits but based on the fall 1994 set of visits.

TRACKING CHANGES OVER TIME AND ORGANIZING DATA

A key theme in RAND's analysis is an examination of the evolution of the designs through time and the reasons for changes to the designs or planned progress. The initial proposals constitute the starting point. The designs evolved through Phase 1 and will continue to evolve through Phase 2. We are interested in documenting the changes that have occurred and the reasons for them.

Whole-school designs potentially incorporate a number of elements. These elements can be used to contrast and compare designs and also as a means to follow changes in designs over time. These elements are related to John Goodlad's notion of school commonplaces or characteristics of schooling that are evident in all schools even though the specific dimensions of those commonplaces might vary among schools.[4] So, for example, all schools have a curriculum, a governance structure, and a way to determine how students are progressing, but the details of these elements vary among schools. Elements are basically ways to define the organization called school and the process called schooling.

After a content analysis of the design documents, we modified the Goodlad commonplaces to fit the NASDC designs and now use a unique set of elements to describe, compare, and contrast the NASDC designs. Although the elements are common simply because they exist in all schools, the teams' relative emphasis on these elements is also a product of the RFP process and the research base that supports educational reform. The NASDC RFP asked that some elements be specifically addressed and that designs reflect America 2000 goals. Thus, because of language in the RFP, all designs describe how they will deal with standards and assessments. Because "all students entering school ready to learn" is a national education goal, all designs address the need for social services to support education in some fashion. Some elements are commonly addressed because a strong research base has led those interested in education to form similar hypotheses about how to improve performance. For example, although the importance of children coming to school ready to learn is one of the national education goals, the need to

---

[4]Goodlad (1984).

provide social support for children and their families is also strongly indicated by a growing literature that was cited by teams as influencing them in constructing their designs.

The elements used in this analysis follow in brief form; each will be further defined in subsequent paragraphs.   We note that the definitions used are broad.   This is to allow for the great variance among designs in the details of the common features.

- **Curriculum and instruction:** These two elements include what knowledge bases are learned and in what sequence, and the manner in which knowledge is transmitted to the student.

- **Standards:**   Range of skills and content areas a student is expected to master to progress through the system and levels of attainment necessary for schools to be judged effective.

- **Assessments:** The means for measuring progress toward standards, either by the schools or by students.

- **Student grouping:**   Criteria or basis for assigning students to classes, groups, or programs.

- **Community involvement:**   How parents, business, and others participate in schools and vice versa.

- **Integration of social services:** How and when social services will be provided for students to be ready to learn.

- **Governance**:   The distribution of authority and responsibility among education actors: states, districts, school members, and others.   School-level governance changes usually increase its participatory nature, district-to-school governance changes usually require site based management, and state-level changes often demand different legal responsibilities for schools and districts or different legal responsibilities among education and noneducation partners.

- **Professional development:** This has at least four components as discussed in team documents. Staff training includes the traditional workshops and inservices provided on particular subjects or issue areas from cooperative learning to emergency procedures. These were often referred to as inservices and were highly specific and time constrained. Professional growth opportunities include opportunities to develop curriculum and instruction, to develop expertise in using standards to develop curriculum, to collaborate with others, and to enter into networks or prolonged discussions with other teachers about the profession. Several teams planned to supplement the above two types of professional development with opportunities for changed practice such as extensive on-the-job practice, coaching in the classroom, and teaming in individual classrooms as well as schoolwide forums to permanently change the ways in which teachers deliver curriculum and instruction. Changed organizational structures and incentives encourage teachers to access both staff inservices and professional growth opportunities.

- **Structure, staffing, and allocation of staff time:** The roles and responsibilities of different staff.

We now turn to the specifics of the designs to compare and contrast them further.

Chapter Four

DESIGNS AND THEIR CHARACTERISTICS

This chapter examines the designs and their elements at the macro level to make some rough comparisons. This chapter should acquaint the reader with the common features and differences among the designs as well as explore the range of the NASDC undertaking. We contrast and compare the designs of the elements identified in the previous chapter to illuminate apparent groupings of designs and point out some simple implications, given the differences.

DESIGNS' APPROACH TO SCHOOL CHANGE

Two characteristics capture the essence of the many differences among designs: the number and type of elements included in the design and the number of collaborators that the design team must have to develop the design at a site (see Figure 4.1).

The core designs tend to place their greatest emphasis for change in a narrow set of elements: curriculum, instruction, standards, assessments, student groupings, community involvement, and professional development. They emphasize school-level partnerships as their main point of entry and continued interaction.

The comprehensive designs tend to emphasize more elements and include integrated social services, governance changes, and organization and staffing changes as important, even distinguishing elements, of the designs. These teams believe that they need to develop and maintain collaborative efforts with actors outside of schools to accomplish these goals. Nevertheless, they still focus on schools as the intervention point of their designs.

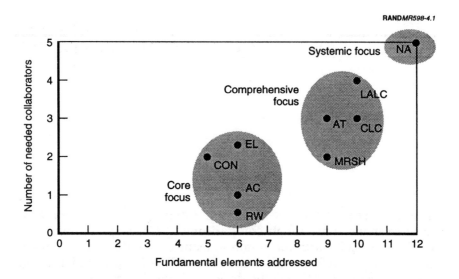

Figure 4.1—Designs and Collaborators Needed for Them

Finally, one team, NA, is taking a more systemic approach. It covers all elements and intends to support collaborative arrangements with many actors in an effort to change the systems that support individual schools. Its point of intervention is at the central office or district level and with other agencies that support schools.

COMPARATIVE BREADTH OF DESIGNS

The design teams contrasted rather sharply in terms of the elements included in their proposals at the end of Phase 1 that each team considered fundamental to its vision of the design.

Content analysis of the proposals, including updated design documents in 1994, as well as interviews with the teams, showed that the teams differed in the inclusion or exclusion of desired changes reflected in the element list and the relative emphasis they put on those elements.

The following paragraphs contrast the designs by element. The results, which indicate elements included in the design at the begin-

ning of Phase 2 based on a document review and discussions with
the design teams, are shown in Figure 4.2. If a team strongly emphasizes an element, we indicate this by using a light grey to show
that the team is focusing on producing something in this element
category. If the team was weaker in an element's emphasis, or if we

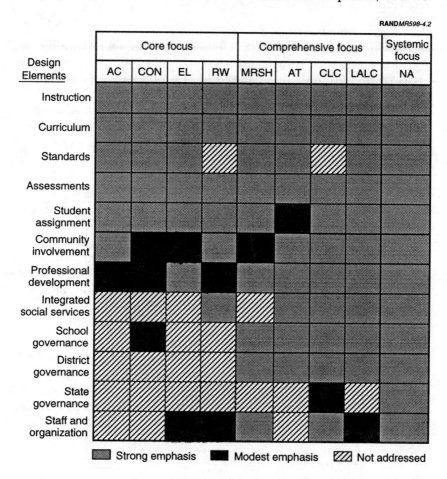

Figure 4.2—Level of Initial Challenge to Design Teams Keyed to Number of
Elements Included

judge it to be a modest change compared to that demanded by other designs, we indicate so with a dark grey. If the design did not address that element the category is indicated with a diagonal hatch.

Curriculum and Instruction

All design teams intend to make significant changes to the elements of curriculum and instruction. There is a general move by all teams toward interdisciplinary, project-based curriculum, in several designs tailored to individual students. Several include service to the community and internships as part of a required curriculum. However, the details of these changes indicate a great deal of variation among teams. Nevertheless, all teams felt that changes in these two elements were fundamental.

Standards

All teams intend to create new standards, of one type or another, except for CLC and RW. These two designs will use existing state standards but will bring all students to those standards. Thus, they do not have the major challenge of creating new standards that other teams do. Two teams (AC and MRSH) are creating their own unique standards, and others are combining existing standards and particular skills to emphasize the concerns of their teams.

Assessments

All teams intend to develop at least performance-based student-level assessments keyed to their standards, curriculum, and instruction. Several talk about systems of assessments. The designs did not distinguish themselves further.

Student Assignment

Seven teams emphasize changes in the assignment of students within schools such as multi-age grouping, multi-year groupings, cooperative learning, and project-based learning in groups. The exceptions are AC and AT. However, although these two teams do not specify particular student groupings, in some ways it could be considered implied by their curriculum and instructional methods.

Community Involvement

Six teams emphasize the need for "greater community involvement" in the school or greater school involvement in the community as a key thrust of the design. For the three others, CON, EL, MRSH, this is noted, but it is not a major emphasis.

Professional Development

Six teams stated that they intend to make fundamental changes to the professional development process for teachers as part of their designs, oftentimes including changes to the role of teachers and to teacher education. Two other teams (AC, RW) do not indicate fundamental changes to the process; rather, they indicate that professional development would change to emphasize significant training in their particular methods.

Integrated Social Services

Five teams place a good deal of emphasis on the provision of integrated social services in schools (AT, CLC, LALC, NA, and RW). AT, CLC, LALC, and NA emphasize the need to make the school the focus of provision, integrating education and social services. RW has a family support coordinator at the school but does not require integrated social services at the school.

School-Level Governance

Five teams (AT, CLC, LALC, MRSH, and NA) require formal changes to school-level governance—usually the setting up of governance committees with participation of teachers and others. CON promotes the creation of two committees, but this is not key to the design. Others encourage these types of changes, but do not require them.

District-School Governance

Five teams require formal and very significant changes to the relationship between the school and district (AT, CLC, LALC, MRSH, and NA). Each of these teams requires significant school-level control over resources, budgeting, and staffing. The other teams promote and encourage this, but do not require it.

State Governance

One team (NA) seeks changes at the state level to promote reform, including formal changes to the responsibilities of the education and social service agencies. CLC implies state-level support for charter schools, but this is not a prerequisite for noncharter school districts in its sample.

Staff and Organization

Finally, three teams emphasize the need for significant, permanent changes to the staff structure, and in fact based their designs on these changes (CLC, MRSH, and NA). Three others are not so emphatic (EL, LALC, and RW).

An interesting pattern emerged from a simple analysis of these relative emphases. Four designs (AC, CON, EL, and RW) place emphasis on and confine themselves primarily to changes in curriculum, instruction, standards, assessments, student assignments, professional development, and community involvement. Five designs (MRSH, AT, CLC, LALC, and NA) cover these elements but heavily emphasize changes to governance, social services, and school organization.

In attempting to identify challenges inherent in the designs, one might ask, "Are specific problems associated with any of the elements that would prevent demonstration within Phase 2?"

The answer is that each element is probably easy to change at a superficial level, but probably very difficult to change at a significant level. Thus, each element poses challenges to the design teams and schools for demonstration in the NASDC timeframe. The issues posed by significant changes to the elements of curriculum, instruction, standards, and assessments appear to be well known, especially at the school-building level. These are faced equally by all teams.

The elements of governance, integrated social services, and organization or structure are clearly identified with "restructuring" reforms. As more schools and districts attempt "restructuring," evidence is accumulating that restructuring, like changes to the core elements, is difficult to accomplish and slow to materialize. Research is beginning to show that slow, nonuniform progress toward changes in these elements can be expected for the following reasons.[1]

- Local context has an overwhelming effect on the ability to demonstrate these reforms.

- These elements are controlled by organizations outside the normal influence of small groups of reformers or of schools.

- The processes to change these elements require complex negotiations by many actors, which are slow and time consuming.

This would lead us to expect that designs with these elements might have further difficulties meeting the NASDC timeframe for demonstration within sites than those without these elements. From the above, one might expect that several designs (AT, CLC, LALC, MRSH, and NA) would face significant additional challenges in this regard because they have more areas in which to demonstrate changes than the other four designs.

NEED FOR COLLABORATION AND PARTNERS

The designs also offered significant contrasts in the emphasis they placed on collaborative efforts with groups outside the design team to demonstrate their designs in schools. Figure 4.3 shows the different types of collaborations (outside the team) that the design teams talk about or require for the further specification and demonstration of their designs.

---

[1] Policy Studies Associates, Inc. (1994); Liberman et al. (1991); and Bimber (1994).

RAND*MR598-4.3*

	AC	AT	CON	CLC	EL	LALC	MRSH	NA	RW
School	X	X	X	X	X	X	X	X	X
District		X		X		X	X	X	
State								X	
Teachers' schools			X		X	X		X	
Social service agencies		X		X		X		X	

Figure 4.3—Collaborative Efforts Required by Teams

Five teams focus almost exclusively on schools and their associated districts as the main point of collaboration in their demonstration efforts (AC, CON, EL, MRSH, RW). Conversations with team members indicate that they place primary emphasis on schools as their partners and think about their contribution to reform as a school-by-school effort.

In contrast, four teams (AT, CLC, LALC, NA) require cooperation or collaboration with actors other than districts—most notably states, teachers' colleges, and social service providers. Conversations with these teams confirm that they place significant emphasis on collaboration with actors external to the school. For NA, these interactions are as, if not more, important than those with individual schools.

We draw a simple inference from this. Those teams with more need for collaboration face a greater challenge in completing the design within the NASDC timeframe. They must develop and specify their design, as well as build and maintain partnerships and influence with more actors to demonstrate their design at sites—a challenge to resources and capabilities.

IMPLICATION OF DESIGN APPROACHES FOR PHASE 2 OUTCOMES

These themes—broadness of element coverage and needed collaboration—merge into three approaches for reform that distinguish the teams as well as form expectations about their ability to meet NASDC goals for Phase 2—full demonstration of the designs in real schools by June 1995.

The core designs (AC, CON, EL, and RW) tend to place their greatest emphasis for change in seven elements: curriculum, instruction, standards, assessments, student groupings, community involvement, and professional development. They emphasize school-level partnerships—it is their main point of entry and continued interaction. As such, the approach is intended to develop a design and team that can help schools make major and direct changes in the core of schooling—what goes on in the classroom.

The comprehensive designs (AT, CLC, LALC, MRSH) tend to emphasize more elements and include integrated social services, governance changes, and organization and staffing changes as fundamental to the design. These teams believe that they need to construct partnerships or collaborative efforts to support the schools. Although a good deal of their efforts will likely go to the development and maintenance of collaborative efforts at reforms, their primary focus is still on individual schools or small clusters of schools.

Finally, one team (NA) has taken a systemic approach, encompassing all elements, and working primarily outside of schools to make these changes.

We expect that comprehensive and systemic designs will face greater challenges than the core designs in terms of meeting the Phase 2 goals of NASDC. A combination of focusing on more elements and needing to manage a greater number of external collaborations or partnerships presents obvious additional challenges to these teams over those faced by the core designs. However, over the long term, these comprehensive and systemic designs might promote fundamental changes needed in school support systems that are the key to reform permanence. By addressing key issues, they might not be able to meet the NASDC Phase 2 deadlines. Nevertheless, their contribution could be great.

Chapter Five

DEVELOPMENT STRATEGIES AND PROCESSES

Those who would reform the educational system are well aware of the difficulties involved in the process of change. Wonderful, but abstract, concepts for schooling have failed to be demonstrated in actual schools as the schools changed the concepts to fit their own circumstances. Past studies of reform efforts have shown that the design as demonstrated was often not the design envisioned and that after diligent efforts at reform, variation within and between schools adopting the same reforms was as great as among schools adopting dissimilar reforms.[1]

This chapter explores the strategies chosen by the design teams to transform the concepts proposed in the responses to the RFP into well-specified and developed designs. The chapter describes the development philosophies of the teams. These are combined to indicate three different approaches to the Phase 2 development evident in the teams activities: a team specified and developed approach; a team specified and site developed approach; and a site specified and developed approach.

RESPONSIBILITY FOR FURTHER DEVELOPMENT IN PHASE 2

Each team had to determine how to go about the further specification and development of the design concepts as well as the imple-

---

[1]Milbrey McLaughlin (1990, p. 12) states this as "Implementation dominates outcome." See also Rivlin and Timpane (1975).

mentation in Phase 2 sites and final implementation in Phase 3 sites. Who would do this work of specifying and developing the designs was an obvious issue facing the teams.

By responsibility for design specification, we mean that someone had to make decisions about what would or would not be included in the design, element by element and within each element. For example, in specifying the design element of new student grouping, someone must decide if the design includes multi-year or multi-age grouping as an essential component of that element. In specifying instructional strategies, someone must determine whether the design demands project-based learning or not. If project-based learning is required, then someone must also decide the relative balance between this type of curriculum and instruction and other types such as didactic pedagogy.

Responsibility for development can be separated from responsibility for specification, although overlaps exist. After a decision that something belongs in the design, someone must develop the artifacts of the design—models, plans, and materials that provide specific details and guide actors in the demonstration and implementation. In the case of project-based learning, someone would be responsible for developing projects down to the lesson-plan level for teachers to use that met the standards of the design. Someone would also have to develop the models of multi-age grouping that would be most appropriate to the design. Do fifth and sixth graders get grouped together or sixth and seventh? Or is the choice made by individual assessment, not age?

In general, the choice of who would be responsible was a choice between the design team or the personnel at the site, usually teachers. In making that choice, design teams, as indicated in proposals and interviews, talked of the "school implementation" literature as guiding their decisions.

THEMES FROM SCHOOL IMPLEMENTATION LITERATURE

The literature described by teams offered a fundamental dilemma to be faced by the teams in the further development of the designs.

Reform Specification and Local Adaptation

Specification of the reform agenda, policies, and practices is crucial to reform. First, full specification is said to be important for successful demonstration or implementation.[2] Poorly specified or underspecified reforms do not provide the level of the organization closest to the student (meaning teachers and schools administrators) with clear direction toward change. Vague mandates for change do not provide personnel with well-defined reform tasks. Operators do not know what they are supposed to do to support the reform and soon fall into old habits.

However, for operating levels that have significant existing autonomy such as classroom teachers, an overly specified design can challenge that autonomy and provoke noncompliance with the intent of the reform. In general, and perhaps specifically with groups having great autonomy, mutual development of the specifics of the reform is thought to lead to more "buy-in" and reduced implementation problems related to operator understanding.[3]

Site-Level Adaptation

Most research talks about demonstration or implementation being site-specific.[4] Local-level factors are bound to affect implementation of any general reform idea. Thus, researchers often talk of a need for local actors to change the design to meet local needs. Note that this is different from the need for buy-in, which calls for adaptation between school-level operators and external mandators of change. Local actors often adapt generalized concepts to fit with local realities. However, if local adaptation runs rampant, as might be the case for a locally specified and developed design, then little change might be forthcoming because the design is held hostage to local politics,

---

[2]This argument is most firmly stated in Mazmanian and Sabatier (1981).

[3]This argument is elaborated in Berman and McLaughlin (1975).

[4]Again summarized by Mazmanian and Sabatier (1981), but demonstrated in Berman and McLaughlin (1975) for education reform and more recently by Bodilly et al. (1993) and Bodilly, Purnell, and Hill (1994). Mirel (1994) provides an insightful case study of the effects of local politics on a reform effort in Bensenville, Illinois, one of the two teams dropped by NASDC after the design year.

local personalities, and local capacity shortfalls or significant change might occur, but not in keeping with the design principles.

School-Level Assistance

A large part of the implementation literature is also concerned with what types of assistance are needed to get people to change their behaviors, including specific models, training, face-to-face coaching, secondary materials, networks, funding, time to develop mutually acceptable reform tasks, etc. The original work of Gross, Giaquinta, and Bernstein (1971) indicated that even though administrators and teachers might be initially highly supportive of a reform concept, this does not directly translate into change.[5] If assistance is not provided, then the reform does not take place. Training and resources are often included in plans for implementation. However, when budgets become tight, training and other resources for change are the first to be cut to preserve current operations. This results in implementation failure.

For complex tasks, simple training routines will not be enough to change behaviors. Instead, strong face-to-face support over time and opportunities for practice in real-life situations are needed to get permanent change in behaviors. Altogether, this adds up to the need for dedicated reform resources from the design teams and districts to schools to demonstrate the design.

Implications

This points to the need for design teams to carefully balance their roles and the roles of the site personnel in further specification and development. On the one hand, a strong team role in both specification and development of the design might provide the clear materials and tasks needed by school personnel to aid in the adoption. This approach, however, runs the risk of a backlash from teachers and problems arising because the design is not appropriate to site-level conditions.

---

[5]Gross, Giaquinta, and Bernstein (1971).

On the other hand, greater local input in specification and development is said to ensure school staff buy-in leading to more permanent commitment to the reform. The staff would in fact mold team guidelines to fit their circumstances. However, this approach might result in large variations across sites in the short run and slow movement toward demonstration. The nonuniform demonstration is due to differences among the sites in their capacity for change and the molding of the design to meet local needs. The slower movement is due to school staff having to develop the design at the same time as they perform their normal work tasks and the possibility that the site reduces the pace of change to suit the locality. (It could also be the case that the site with extraordinary capability increases the pace of change.)

APPROACHES TO RELATIVE RESPONSIBILITY FOR DEVELOPMENT IN PHASE 2

Interviews with the design teams and a review of the proposals indicated that all had given deliberate thought to the dilemma faced concerning the relative responsibility of the team and the sites in further specification and development. All teams talked in terms of organizational change being more likely if a flexible, mutual adjustment process was used. They avoided highly prescribed designs or mandatory styles of implementation. All teams used at least some aspects of a prototype development where the design is expected to evolve as the schools and design teams respond to each other and move together toward improved levels of performance. Each team talked of its design unfolding or evolving with practical experiences. Although a common approach is apparent, at least when compared to some past top-down reform efforts, the teams tended to cluster around different development strategies that will likely affect the demonstration experience as shown in Figure 5.1.

Team Specified and Developed

One group of teams, including AC and RW, is more reliant on the capabilities of the design teams to fully specify and develop the design. These two teams, in contrast with others, had existing standards,

RANDMR598-5.1

		Design team	Local site
Responsibility for developing models, curriculum, materials	Local site	CON EL LALC MRSH	AT CLC NA
	Design team	AC RW	

Responsibility for specifying elements

Figure 5.1—Teams' Different Approaches to Development

curriculum, and instructional models and had demonstrated parts of these models before the effort.[6] Their proposals to NASDC are comparatively specific about what is and what is not included. Their intention is to work with the schools to further develop the designs, but the teams themselves carry the burden of responsibility for most of the development. At a minimum, the teams will provide the standards (or, for RW, have them provided by the state partner, Maryland), curriculum frameworks, models of lesson plans, list of resources, models for student assignment, and assessment in keeping with the specific elements of the design. Teachers will experiment and use these models and provide feedback during the Phase 2 period, oftentimes developing pieces of the specific curriculum (AC teachers develop their own lesson plans using the frameworks and models provided). The design team will then adapt the design and supporting materials to be more user friendly.

Expectations for this group should be that, assuming the team has the capabilities needed, the further specification and development of the design should go smoothly. The design team tasks are clearly laid out, no negotiations need take place as to relative responsibility, and

---

[6]AC developed its own standards in keeping with other national ones, but RW adopted the Maryland state standards and developed curriculum to meet those standards.

school staff are being asked to add minimal additional tasks to their routine ones. (AC does ask for lesson plan development and this is not minimal in the sense of work involved, but minimal when compared to what is being asked by other design teams.) Issues might arise, after development, as the team attempts to get sites to implement the design. It is then that backlashes that might prevent implementation would occur. If this occurred, the design team would have a well-specified and well-developed set of materials, and weak demonstration sites.

In the future (Phase 3) the intentions of these teams is to offer comparatively specified and detailed designs to schools, with expert assistance in the implementation of the designs.

Locally Specified and Developed

In contrast, another set of teams, including AT, CLC, and NA, will provide primarily principles and resources to schools and guide the schools through a process of improvement where the schools specify and develop their own designs in keeping with general guidelines. For example, NA will provide a set of standards for the schools to work with, a set of tasks to undertake such as the development of a school improvement plan and a plan to work with local social service providers, and some resources for undertaking these tasks. The resources tend to be access to experts, conferences, and written materials that will expose school staff to new ideas.

AT has a sequential process that schools must go through to transform themselves. For example, the district must set up an autonomous pathway (feeder pattern with elementary, middle, and high schools serving students in a geographic area) governed by a representative team, and the pathway school must set up new governing committees. These committees will then begin to transform the schools with the aid of the design team. Again, the team provides resources such as access to experts and printed materials. Meanwhile the schools specify what they will become and begin to develop the means to do so. Thus, in contrast to the team development model, the sites develop their own standards, curriculum, and instruction and choose what kind of student groupings are appropriate. The governance structure is, however, specified by the team.

Given this approach, one might expect that progress toward full development of the design will vary by site as each site makes decisions about what transformation means in the local context. Much of the further development of the design, from principles to practical artifacts, will depend on local capabilities which vary across sites. Because the site chooses the path of reform and the pace of change in accordance with its needs and capabilities, one might expect slow progress toward fuller development or at least a rate of progress that varies. Progress toward local development will be closely tied to the ability to free site-level developers from routine tasks such as teaching. This approach requires that the design team and the site clearly understand at the beginning of the effort that the site is responsible for the uniquely local development of this design.

This site diversity and slow pace will not diminish in Phase 3. The intention of these teams is to use local development as the primary means to reform.

Design Team Specified with Local Development

A final group of teams, including CON, EL, LALC, and MRSH, intend to take major responsibility in specifying the design, but will rely on the sites to further develop the models, curriculum, assessments, assignments, etc. These teams have already specified subelements of the design as evidenced in the proposal and design documents through 1994. On the other hand, the demonstration sites are expected to further develop many of these elements. For example, CON requires the school to reorganize into multi-year and multi-age groupings, use a project-based curriculum, use CON specified and developed standards, and have specific computer supports. The site, given materials and staff inservices on the topics, decides and develops its unique multi-year and multi-age grouping plan, develops a curriculum framework, develops an entirely new curriculum based on projects, and revises the CON-developed standards to meet local needs.

Although the elements to be further developed by the site differ among these teams, CON, EL, and MRSH hold in common that teachers must go through the process of curriculum development as part of their professional growth. They believe that the process of matching standards, assessments, curriculum, and instruction into a coherent whole not only builds expertise but promotes teacher commitment to the curriculum changes. Teachers will not abandon what they themselves have developed. In addition, although these teams have specified that multi-age or multi-year groupings are a part of the design, they have not developed the exact model to use. In Phase 2, demonstration sites will experiment with different approaches.

Like the locally specified and developed model, further development of the design in Phase 2 will depend on the capabilities of the schools. Thus, one should expect slow progress with significant variation among sites. The sites will not be responsible for specifying the design, but they will be responsible for much of the development of materials, models, curriculum, etc. Unless staff are freed from other tasks, this development will be slow.

These teams' expectations for Phase 3 is that the development effort would be largely complete and that new sites would not undertake the heavy development load of the demonstration sites. However, CON, EL, and MRSH, which believe in teacher creation of curriculum as part of a step in professional development, will always include this "developmental" activity. Even so, teachers at Phase 3 schools presumably would be aided by fully developed models, materials, and example lessons from the Phase 2 sites.

ROUTINE SCHOOL REFORM PROBLEMS

Regardless of who is responsible for the specification and development of the design, routine problems affect every school improvement effort. They are problems not peculiar to any design approach but to the school environment. The literature illustrates the difficulty of completing social reforms because of what might be considered routine organizational occurrences in politically fragmented environments.[7] With or without a reform agenda, leaders leave schools and districts, budgets are cut, taxpayers revolt and impose tax caps, inclement weather or natural disasters strike schools, and courts is-

---

[7]Mazmanian and Sabatier (1981) provide a list of some of these gathered from others work. Case studies by Bodilly et al. (1993) and Bodilly, Purnell, and Hill (1994) provide some recent examples of the effects of routine mishaps on reform efforts.

sue decrees. In "normal times" these common occurrences can cause havoc in schools. In "reform times," these occurrences have unpredictable effects on the pace and direction of the reform. For example, leadership turnover might sound like a disaster, but in fact new leadership might be even more supportive of reform. Although these situations are unpredictable in nature, reforms must deal with their realities and must have plans for ameliorating their effects.

All teams have already felt the pressures of budget constraints and slow progress toward important agreements between design teams and districts due to political or other disruptions. For example, LALC's site efforts began in the midst of major restructuring efforts in the Los Angeles Unified School District (LAUSD) and at a time when voters were considering partitioning the district. Because the district and union are partners in the design, these issues had to be worked out before parts of the design could move forward.

In several cases, designs have faced the additional challenge of creating new schools from scratch—a formidable task. Both CLC and EL have sites that are establishing new schools in existing buildings, hiring teachers, buying equipment and materials, and marketing the school to prospective students and their parents. The actions and energies involved in setting up schools can drain energy away from the reform efforts and need to be considered in examining the implementation of the design.

IMPLICATIONS FOR NASDC EFFORT

Expectations for fuller development of the designs by the end of Phase 2 should take into account the approach taken by the team. Those teams relying on local specification or development can be expected to proceed toward fuller development according to the capabilities of the sites, and local variation should be expected. Teams using these strategies might be more vulnerable to disruptions in school that draw the attention of school staff away from reform. This site-based development in Phase 2 will affect the ability to demonstrate the design. Sites that are slow to pursue their responsibilities will also be slow to demonstrate.

Teams that intend to take major responsibility for both specification and development will likely show more rapid progress toward fuller development of the design. However, these teams run the risk of slow progress at demonstration sites if teachers do not accept the designs. Their challenge is to provide the assistance needed for teachers to adopt the design-team-developed models and materials.

Chapter Six

DESIGN TEAM READINESS

The design teams did not come to NASDC equally equipped to meet the demands for rapid development, demonstration, and then scale-up. Many factors affected their readiness to undertake the NASDC effort. We draw contrasts between the teams on four factors: whether the team was newly created, whether it needed to build a staff and structure to undertake the effort, whether the leadership of the team had to develop or be transferred, and whether the team or team members as a group lacked experience in implementation of school-level reform. These four factors intertwine in the sense that a newly created team would have to build staff and develop leadership, whereas an existing one might have a staff and structure already in place.[1]

It appears reasonable to expect that teams facing the challenges involved in team-building and lacking experience at reform would make slower progress in Phase 2 than those teams that were on sound footing in terms of staff and structure as well as having strong implementation experience. Newly created teams would have to address team building and capacity issues before working with sites toward demonstration. This is a difficult, resource-consuming task.

We have summarized the standing of the different teams at the end of Phase 1 in terms of these factors in Figure 6.1. Teams that faced many challenges in any of these areas were given a diagonal hatch;

---

[1]A fifth and important factor is missing from the discussion: the level of design team funding by NASDC. As stated previously, the level of funding varied dramatically among teams.

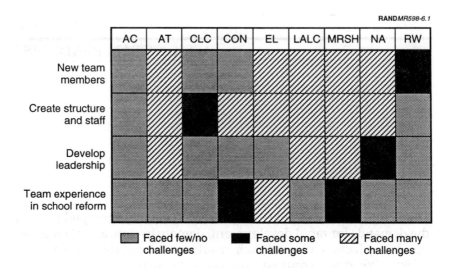

Figure 6.1—Teams' Various Challenges to Build Capability in Year 1

teams with some modest challenges were given black, and teams with few or no challenges in this regard were given grey.

These four factors and their potential effect are explored below. Finally, we add that several teams had disruptions in their funding streams in Phase 1 that left them less ready for initiating Phase 2 activities.

NEW TEAMS OR TEAM MEMBERS

The creation of a new team implies that the first year of the NASDC effort, and maybe other years as well, would have to be devoted to developing the team and its common vision, taking energy away from actual work at the demonstration sites. Already existing teams would be less likely to face this challenge and could begin the work of development and demonstration immediately. Therefore, teams that were newly created organizations with no prior experience working together would face the additional challenge in Phase 2 of team-building and could be expected, all other things equal, to progress more slowly.

Three teams (AC, CLC, and CON—the latter sponsored by Bolt, Beranek, and Newman) existed before the effort as school-change organizations, and the members of the existing organizations were largely responsible for the proposals and will be responsible for the development work.

Two other teams (NA and RW) existed before the RFP as school-change organizations, but have had changes in team memberships during the RFP process or during Phase 1. In the case of RW, the Success For All program of Johns Hopkins joined with the State of Maryland and St. Mary's County to become Roots and Wings, but Johns Hopkins remained the team lead and is synonymous with Roots and Wings (black in Figure 6.1). In the case of NA, the parent organization of the National Center on Education and the Economy and the National Alliance concept existed before the effort, but new partners were involved in responding to the RFP.

Four teams were created in large part to respond to the NASDC RFP including AT, EL, LALC, and MRSH. Although they had preexisting "parent organizations," the birth of the design team corresponds closely to the time of the NASDC initiative. For example, the Hudson Institute is the parent organization of Modern Red Schoolhouse, but MRSH was created by Hudson in partnership with others to address the NASDC proposal and Hudson had little school experience. Outward Bound, the parent organization of EL, existed and was beginning to help selected schools reform, but the EL team was pulled together in earnest to respond to the proposal. We expect that these teams will face additional challenges in the Phase 2 period (diagonal hatch on Figure 6.1).

STAFF BUILDING AND ORGANIZATIONAL STRUCTURE

A major task for the NASDC effort is to develop a staff capable of helping schools demonstrate the design and, in Phase 3, implement the design. New organizations or small organizations geared to a more modest effort would face the challenge of building a staff and creating the structure with which the organization could work effectively with sites.

Two pre-existing teams (AC and RW) had such staff and implementation structures in place. On the face of it, the additional number of sites undertaken in the demonstration do not pose major challenges to the existing staff and structure of these teams. They will have to grow modestly, but they do not appear to face a major challenge (grey on Figure 6.1).

Another preexisting team (CLC) faces a more significant growth challenge. Its preexisting structure included only the four principals. Working in over five sites would require the team to increase staff and to develop assistance structures (black on Figure 6.1).

Obviously, the newly created teams (AT, EL, LALC, and MRSH) face the full challenge of developing the staff and the structure to assist schools. In addition, two other teams (CON and NA) must significantly increase their staff and intervention structures from those existing at the beginning of the NASDC effort. This is most keenly felt by NA, which includes as sites multiple states, districts, and schools. (All six are indicated by a diagonal hatch on Figure 6.1.)

DEVELOP NEW LEADERSHIP

Although the development of leadership is necessary to all teams, often the issue is solved during the creation of the team. The team leaders are those who created the team. However, in several cases those who created the organization and responded to the RFP were not the ones destined to lead the organization. Discussions in Phase 1 indicated that the hand-off of leadership responsibility or the assignment of leadership responsibility will be an issue for several teams.

For most teams this has not been an issue (AC, CLC, CON, EL, and RW). The leadership has been clear from the start and remains so, even though the relative functions of different leaders shifted in Phase 1.

For three teams (AT, LALC, and MRSH), this has been a major issue. In the case of AT and MRSH, the leaders who presented the proposal are not the same as those who now lead the development and demonstration effort. The organizational growth required that leadership be handed off to someone from outside the original organization. For example, the four founding organizations of AT turned over their managerial responsibility to a newly hired director at the end of

Phase 1. At LALC, several members of the design team were replaced: deputy director of LALC, the Los Angeles Unified School District Superintendent, and district budget chief. A recurring issue is the assignment of a director who can take charge of the effort and manage the day-to-day realities of school reform issues. Political leaders abound on the team, but not administrative leaders.

Finally, NA faces some modest challenges in this regard because of leadership turnover in Phase 1. One of the leaders left and was replaced by two co-leaders who were already familiar with the design and the other members.

NATURE OF TEAM EXPERIENCE IN SCHOOL REFORM

The teams also brought significantly different levels of experience in school reform to the effort. Teams with less direct experience in designing, developing, and demonstrating in real schools would face greater challenges, all other things equal, than those with strong hands-on experiences.

Six teams had strong backgrounds in this area (AC, AT, CLC, LALC, NA, and RW). In each of these cases, the team itself had implemented school changes in the past (AC and RW) or principal leaders brought this experience to the team (AT, CLC, LALC, and NA).

Two other teams faced some modest challenges in this regard. Both CON and MRSH had more limited school implementation experience than the others.

In contrast with all others, EL had the least experience in this field. A newly created team, whose parent organization is Outward Bound, had only recently entered into the area of school reform. Several members had school experience, but it was not equivalent to the deliberate reform efforts of the other teams.

FUNDING ISSUES

The strategy outlined in the NASDC RFP was predicated upon a funding level of $150 million to $200 million over five years. Design teams were encouraged to submit proposals that were not limited by funding constraints. However, as time went on it became clear that initial estimates of fund-raising capabilities were too ambitious—a shortfall in predicted revenues would occur.

In the negotiations between design teams and NASDC in summer 1992 to develop contracts for the effort and again in 1993, design teams were forced to rethink their design in light of reduced funding.

The measures each team took varied, but two approaches were fairly common. First, most cut back immediately on the technology element of the design. Fewer funds would be available to cover the cost of hardware and software for the schools. One consequence might be limited ability of the designs to implement strongly individualized curriculum and instructional strategies because the technological means to schedule and manage individual students might not be available. Second, several design teams cut back on the number of implementation sites or pushed into the future any consideration of adding sites.

This process affected all teams in some form or other, but three teams had an additional problem to deal with that can be expected to affect demonstration progress. These teams (AT, CLC, and MRSH) had contractual arrangements geared to the school year. Their plans for summer 1993 staff development and orientation sessions for the sites were grounded on the expectation of signing Phase 2 contracts in spring 1993. However, the funding and the contracts covering Phase 2 were slow to develop. Thus, these three teams had difficulty both planning for and implementing the summer orientation and development sessions with the sites that would be crucial to a smooth start-up. Interviews with these teams and their sites indicate that although the three teams scrambled to cover the summer sessions, they could not mount the effort each felt was needed. In turn, site-level interviews indicated for some that this caused problems with establishing good initial relationships with sites.

IMPLICATIONS FOR PHASE 2 EXPECTATIONS

The above discussion indicates that the teams face different challenges in Phase 2 emanating from their readiness at start-up, regardless of the nature of the designs or the approach taken to further specification and development.

Two teams (AC and RW) started the effort with existing and capable staff with strong school reform experiences. We would expect these teams to face few challenges in building the capability needed to demonstrate their designs in Phase 2. We note that these teams moved into their demonstration sites in Phase 1 and began the demonstration effort.

Two other teams (CON and NA) have some challenges to face in this regard, especially the building of a staff and structure for school-level intervention. Although CLC faces fewer challenges in regards to team-building and capability, it had less funding available at the beginning of Phase 2 with which to further develop the design and move into schools.

Finally, four teams (AT, EL, LALC, and MRSH) face Phase 2 with significant challenges regarding their readiness, when compared to the other teams. One should expect that these teams might be slower to proceed than the others and will have more difficulties meeting the NASDC deadlines for Phase 2.

Chapter Seven

THE CHOICE OF DEMONSTRATION SITES

Discussion of the specific nature of each site that the teams chose to work with in Phase 2 of the NASDC effort is beyond the scope of this report. Instead, we limit the discussion to two themes: the choice of number and type of sites and the approach taken to gain initial buy-in from the Phase 2 schools.

NUMBER AND TYPES OF SITES

The decision about the number and types of sites could prove to be crucial to demonstration in Phase 2. Several pitfalls could be possible. Working with one or two sites might focus resources but would also put a team at risk that some local circumstance could easily stall the effort. Working with many sites might dilute the resources of the team and its ability to affect the sites. Working with "highly challenged" sites—those in inner cites with low performance records, might prove to be more difficult than working with "less challenged" sites, those in suburbs with stronger past performance. However, working with such sites might also have a greater potential for showing measurable progress. Teams needed to balance these concerns to ensure at least one, if not more, working demonstration sites by the end of Phase 2.

A review of the decisions made by the teams shows that the choices resulted in three groups.

Modest Portfolio Approach

Four teams chose a modest number of schools to work with, between three and 20 (AC, AT, EL, and RW) and their sample of sites included schools of varying demographics and settings. These teams included a mix of schools with large percentages of children on free and reduced lunch, poor past performances, and in very urban and rural settings as well as some schools with fewer children on free or reduced-price lunch, better performances, and in more suburban settings.

Two other teams (CLC and MRSH) started out with intentions to demonstrate in significantly more sites, but in Phase 1 reduced the number of sites for demonstration in Phase 2 to a modest number in keeping with the others using this approach.

A modest number of schools of varying backgrounds potentially increases the likelihood that at least one of them will have a high payoff in terms of demonstration.

All the Eggs in One Basket Approach

In contrast, two teams (CON and LALC) went with two schools each. All schools in their samples are inner-city schools serving high portions of poverty-level families. As with most inner cities, Boston and Los Angeles are prone to district-level upheavals, which have a high likelihood of affecting the progress of the two design teams. Although the approach focuses the resources of these teams on a limited set of nearby schools, the ability to demonstrate rests entirely on success in two schools in troubled districts.

Large Number Approach

NA was more ambitious in the number of sites involved in Phase 2. Its NASDC efforts cover partnerships with seven states, 25 districts, and 81 schools, with roll-out to more schools during Phase 3. This approach will require extensive resources and capabilities on the part of the team and runs an obvious risk of producing little change across many sites, although the wider coverage increases the odds that at least a few sites will succeed.

SITE SELECTION PROCESS

The process of selection and commitment of sites to work with had two chronological components: a search for likely sites, and the establishment of initial relationships and expectations. These did not vary in any systematic pattern among design teams. Below we describe the general nature of the process.

The Search Process

For the most part, the design teams identified potential sites in a similar manner. The design teams tend to have nationally known reformers as members and these members have networks of sites with whom they have long-standing relationships. The teams, quite naturally, searched among those sites that they were familiar with, had worked with before, or where they had colleagues or friends in the school or district. Design teams have explained that this search method was due to the time constraints imposed by NASDC, the desire to work with familiar people, and the lack of funds in early stages to mount more vigorous searches. But design teams gave additional reasons for working with some schools. Most common was that the school was already implementing elements of the design and thus would be more likely to meet the deadlines set by NASDC. In addition, design teams actively looked for diversity among the sites in terms of students' characteristics and geographic location. For teams with just two sites this was not possible.

The general method of search and selection was the same, but the specifics varied.

- Two teams chose their schools before the proposal was submitted, relying on working relationships with representatives at the district or state levels (CON and RW).

- Four teams requested that interested schools, from a pool of familiar ones, submit an application to be considered for involvement with the implementation effort (EL, CLC, LALC, and MRSH). This did not prohibit the district from strongly influencing the selection.

- Three teams relied on prior affiliations to choose the district to work with, if not the actual schools (AC, AT, and NA). AC worked with the district, but chose the schools based on its own criteria. AT chose districts it was familiar with and the district chose the feeder pattern. NA allowed representatives of its states and districts to choose the individual schools in which to implement, a process that generally involved the submittal of proposals by interested schools.

On the one hand, one might argue that using sites where a relationship existed would allow swifter demonstration, assuming a commitment existed. However, this assumes that commitment is a one-time event, over and done with at the beginning of the effort. We have no reason to expect this to be true. A prior relationship might speed along initiating the design, but continual support and assistance would be necessary to maintain progress.

Initiating the Relations

Once potential sites were identified, the design teams began initiating relationships. In four cases this relationship evolved primarily at the state or district level (AT, CON, MRSH, and NA). Negotiations over the design and plans for demonstration were largely between the design team and district officials or in the case of NA sometimes with state officials. Teachers were not directly consulted by the design team until well into the development year.

In the remainder of the design teams, although initial connections and discussions might have been made at the district level, a more extensive amount of discussion and deliberation occurred between the design team and teachers to ensure commitment (AC, CLC, EL, LALC, and RW). Design team members visited schools, answered questions, and in some cases interviewed teachers to determine the level of commitment to the design and to familiarize themselves with the schools. Teachers and also community members were often involved with the discussions about whether or not to participate in the design implementation.

Most teams attempted to ensure early teacher support in some fashion. First, some arranged for all teachers who did not support adopting the design to be able to leave the school and find employment elsewhere in the district without loss of seniority or status (LALC, MRSH, and RW). Second, some asked the teachers to vote on whether or not to join the effort and asked for a majority of the teachers to vote for the design before proceeding (AT, CLC, EL, LALC, MRSH, and RW). Interviews with sites showed that this process was not consistent among schools associated with any single design team. For example, some AT schools did have a teacher vote and others did not. The same is true for the other designs.

For the most part, design teams were dissatisfied with the unevenness and chaotic nature of the school-level process for ensuring initial buy-in. Most teams have suggested that the Phase 3 process be more deliberate and include more teacher-level orientation and formal voting.

Design teams had one set of reasons for selecting sites, and school personnel had their own reasons for wanting to become involved. School administrators and teachers cited the following reasons for becoming involved, given in the general order of the importance attached by the school members:

- additional financial resources given directly to the school,

- new technology provided by the design team,

- association with a reputable reform movement that would give the school the political clout to effect greater changes,

- access to experts and cutting-edge education reform practices, and

- association with well-known figures who could provide national recognition.

When questioned about their commitment, teachers stated that when they voted, they considered what they would receive from the design team. Few said that they considered what they would be required to do and contribute as a result of their involvement with the design. In general, teachers said they did not have a good understanding of the design or the work they would be required to do when commitment was made, even in those schools that had more extensive introductions to the design teams. They said the design partnership was presented, usually by the principal, as a way of getting funding and experts into the school and that is what teachers approved.

This general reporting of teachers about how they were approached holds true for team-developed as well as co-developed designs. Many school personnel did not know that they would be responsible for a large part of the development of the design. Again, teams voiced dissatisfaction with this and now would require more extensive introductions to ensure better understanding between teams and schools about the relative work involved in transforming the schools.

This chaotic process might not have ensured strong initial buy-in from all school staff, but it does not preclude commitment to the design. Commitment can grow while going through the change process. We saw evidence of strong teacher commitment at many sites, even though the teachers say they did not initially understand or buy into the design.[1]

CHANGES IN SITES

By the end of Phase 1, several of the schools originally affiliated with a NASDC design were no longer involved with the teams. The specific reasons for separating varied, but most can be summed up as a lack of buy-in or commitment on the part of the school or district to the design and its elements. Under such circumstances, the partnerships were dissolved. Specific reasons for dissolution included combinations of the following:

- The school agreed to implement only part of the design, wanting to ignore essential components.

- The local teachers' union expressed strong opposition to various components of the design.

- The school or district disagreed with the design team about resource allocations among the sites.

- The school initially misunderstood the required level of effort and did not want to continue.

- Champions or leaders left and the rest of the staff became disinterested.

---

[1]McLaughlin (1990) discusses this phenomenon.

These experiences to date indicate that getting districts and schools to commit to demonstrate innovative, whole-school designs for Phase 2 was not a simple task. The difficulties were compounded by the demand by some teams that sites act as co-developers. We note that schools initially associated with AC and RW, the teams relying on a team specified and developed approach, have remained with those teams. Clearly, the co-development undertaking involves quite a bit of work, which some schools do not want to perform. In addition, the designs themselves might not appeal to all schools— local tastes, past experiences, and current funding pictures might all affect whether or not a school finds the design compelling and worth its while to pursue. Finally, initial buy-in during Phase 2 will not determine the final outcome. Commitment can be fleeting in organizations with turnover in leadership, fragmented authority structures, and changing circumstances.

IMPLICATIONS FOR PHASE 2 AND PHASE 3

For the most part, we can expect no implications for Phase 2 or Phase 3 in the choice of sites. The selection process tended to be jumbled and somewhat chaotic because of NASDC's ambitious deadlines. The teams did choose different numbers of sites and this might affect their ability to demonstrate their concepts in Phase 2, with CON, LALC, and NA being most at risk of being affected by local circumstances or not having the resources to produce strong demonstration sites. Progress in Phase 3 will, of course, depend on sites chosen for that effort and any lessons the design teams learned from the initial selection for Phase 2.

Chapter Eight

CONCLUSIONS

The following summarizes the implications for Phase 2 of this analysis and also indicates some implications for Phase 3.

CONCLUSIONS AND IMPLICATIONS FOR PROGRESS IN PHASE 2

The discussion in the previous chapters can be summarized simply. The design teams and their designs varied along several dimensions: design characteristics, development approaches, readiness of the team, and site selection decisions. This variance is at least a partial base for expectations about progress in Phase 2.

Teams with core designs (fewer elements and those focused on the school), a team specification and development approach, strong indications of readiness, and a modest number of sites are more likely to emerge from Phase 2 with well-developed designs and strong demonstration sites. Two teams fit this description: AC and RW.

Teams with three or more of the following will likely show slower progress, and this progress will vary significantly from school to school: comprehensive or systemic designs (designs that cover more elements including governance changes, integrated social services, and staffing changes), local specification and development, challenges in terms of readiness, and concentration in a few schools or in many schools. Three teams fit this description: AT, LALC, and NA.

A group of teams falls somewhere between these two extremes, having some challenges (CON, EL, MRSH, and CLC). All required signifi-

in the extent to which they address these issues. Again, some districts will be more amenable to these changes than others and should be sought out for scale-up.

DESCRIPTIONS OF DESIGNS

The following descriptions of the designs rely primarily on the elements defined in Chapter Two. The elements are used as appropriate. The design teams described their designs in 50-page documents and dedicated the development year to specifying the details of the designs. Although these brief paragraphs do not do justice to the designs, we hope they capture some of the essential traits of each.

AUTHENTIC TEACHING, LEARNING, AND ASSESSMENT FOR ALL STUDENTS (AT)

This design assumes that high-performing schools are not possible in the current bureaucratic structure. The intent of the design is to move schools away from "the bureaucratic reality to the authentic vision" of education. The design aims to change the culture of the schools to promote high institutional and individual performance. Four beliefs about the purpose of schools drive the design. Schools are to:

- help students acquire valuable habits of heart, mind, and work,

- help students develop deep understandings,

- use only activities that are developmentally appropriate, and

- create a community of learners.

tem. For example, kindergarten is dedicated to the exploration of "We build a family-school partnership" and "We care for living things." Embedded in each purpose are content areas such as English and math, and essential skills such as critical thinking and researching. Each purpose culminates in a constructive action taken on by the class to serve the community. These fundamental changes in the curriculum and instruction become the organizing principles for all other school activities. The total effect is intended to make the school and its programs more coherent and focused.

Design Team Leaders: Audrey Cohen and Janith Jordan.

Governance: Does not require significant governance changes other than those given to magnet or theme schools. However, significant governance changes can result from the incorporation of purposes as the focus of schooling.

Standards: The school will meet existing state standards, but every school will also have the standards developed by the Audrey Cohen College that align and support the purpose-driven curriculum.

Assessments: Although schools continue to use existing standardized tests as required by the district and state, the design team has also developed a framework of demonstrable abilities and skills for each grade. Teacher-developed assessments are embedded in the curriculum and match the specific purpose of each semester. The team is currently working with the sites to develop results-based assessment criteria and strategies that incorporate community participation.

Student Grouping: Students will be grouped in ways appropriate to the purpose and constructive action of each semester. The curriculum is intended to promote learning of all students.

Curriculum and Instruction: During each semester, students focus all learning and activities on a single pre-assigned purpose. Traditional subject areas and important skills are absorbed by action-oriented dimensions: acting with purpose, weighing values and ethics, understanding self and others, understanding systems, and making use of skills. The semester culminates in a constructive action that has been determined by the students and is directed toward improving the world outside the classroom.   Secondary students serve internships in the community.

Professional Development: The team will provide continued development of teachers in the constructs of the design. Teachers, principals, and administrators organize their jobs around the purposes and begin to build bridges between the school and the outside world.

Community Involvement: The purposes help the school and its officials identify key community resources to involve in the educational enterprise. The constructive actions help bring the community into the school and the school into the community—making schools, parents, and children active partners in improving the community.

Integrated Social Services: The design specifies that coordination with community and health service agencies is accomplished at the site level. The curriculum makes student awareness of health issues and contact with health-related agencies an organic part of the curriculum.

Staffing: The design requires the creation of a staff resource position to gather materials and make contacts in the community, peer-coach teachers in the classroom, and serve as a liaison with the design team. Teachers are responsible for planning the curriculum as a collaborative team. Administrators remove barriers to making the school more coherent and build bridges to the community to support the purposes.

Technology: Networked classroom computer centers, studios for television and photography, and other technology provide students access to information and the means for developing work products. Technology is also applied to the management of record-keeping tasks.

THE CO-NECT SCHOOL DESIGN (CON)

This design calls for a dramatically different learning environment for students, teachers, and the community. The design is especially targeted at middle school children in urban settings; however, it can be applied to other grades and settings. In addition to understanding key subject areas, graduates of the Co-NECT schools demonstrate

directly to its sites to support front-end needs for capital and to promote professional development.

Standards: The design does not propose the development of a unique set of standards, but insists that all students be held to the same standards that emphasize the demonstration of competencies or performances. These results-based standards are intended to be explicit, meaningful, and measurable. The design pledges to ensure that all students have a 75 percent competency rating on existing Minnesota tests and that all students move 25 percentile points on standard measures. The design does promote a standard for ethics as an essential part of character development. This will be developed through close interaction between the student, the school, and the community.

Assessments: It focuses on the more effective use of different assessment techniques to ensure school accountability, teacher accountability, and accurate student assessment. It proposes that five different types of assessments be used to fulfill these different functions. Assessment of students will be more performance-based and move away from seat-time requirements.

Student Grouping: The design uses flexible groupings appropriate to the learning tasks. It will emphasize multi-age, multi-year groupings with few pull-outs.

Curriculum and Instruction: The design keeps traditional subjects, such as English, math, history, and science, while it promotes more interdisciplinary, project-based curriculum and higher-order thinking skills. The point is not to invent new curriculum but to deliver it in ways that make it meaningful to children (instructional strategies). The curriculum emphasizes civic responsibility with students becoming proactive in their communities. The curriculum does not require specific changes but would evolve using modern instructional strategies to be quite different from the current Carnegie units. As such, the design requires working with the university system to create new college entry requirements.

A major focus of the design is on the development of new instructional strategies guided by modern principles of learning that call for "brain-based learning" and when implemented will dramatically increase the learning of all children. It talks of a paradigm shift from "teaching" to "learning" with student-centered instruction and students being responsible for planning their own curriculum. CLC schools would have a Personal Learning Plan (PLP) for each student, emphasize competency-based education, promote contextual learning and applied real-life problem-solving in areas of interest to the child, pay attention to learning styles and the emotional aspects of learning, and maximize the effective use of technology. Multiple forms of exploration and expression would be used to increase the likelihood of learning.

Professional Development: The design makes strong statements about the need for autonomy to support differentiated staffing and alternative certification to meet the twin goals of equal or less cost than other schools, and an increased staff-to-student ratio required by "brain-based" instructional strategies. Teachers develop professional learning plans in conjunction with a schoolwide plan. Each school must commit to giving every teacher 20 days of training a year.

Community Involvement: Schools would be open 24 hours per day to serve adults as well as students. The design has facilities plans to translate this into a reality with different learning stations located throughout the building. As part of this effort, the team works with the media to increase the attention paid to academic achievement in CLC communities. A collaborative approach is encouraged.

Integrated Social Services: A major thrust is that schools become community centers for learning. Social services would be collocated and coordinated through the schools with special emphasis on preschool services to ensure that children are ready to learn.

Staffing: The intent is for schools to use their autonomy over internal resources to significantly restructure the staff and substitute instructional aides or volunteers for teachers. Older students will guide younger students in their studies.

Technology: The design requires substantial use of computers for student assignment and PLP management, for tracking assessments, and for individualized instructional strategies. Computers and other technologies are used in an integral manner to support learning.

and resources, performance assistance, and sufficient time to do what needs to be done.

Design Team Leaders: Peggy Funkhouser, Harry Handler, and Chris Gutierrez.

Partnership: The Los Angeles Educational Partnership (LAEP), a nonprofit organization dedicated to the reform of public education, was the convener of the design team. This design team is unique among NASDC design teams because its leadership includes the Superintendent of the Los Angeles Unified School District (LAUSD) and the President of the United Teachers of Los Angeles (UTLA), and LAEP.

In addition, the design team includes the Senior Vice President of KCET (local PBS station); UCLA and its Center for Research and Evaluation, Standards and Student Testing (CRESST); USC; LEARN leadership; five corporate partners; exemplary teachers; activist parent leaders; and a principal implementing site-based management. LAEP is the fiscal and project manager for the effort.

Governance: Governance is based on participatory democracy, collaboration, and sound management. Each learning center is expected to convene a Town Hall for discussion and to elect a site-based Management Council. The management council is the decisionmaking body for budget, personnel, curriculum, community relations, and student rights, and conducts the annual performance review for the Chief Educational Officer (CEO). Learning centers will be supplied with software to support fiscal management.

Standards: The design will make use of the "highest and most nationally recognized" available standards.

Assessment: CRESST will design a comprehensive student assessment system to improve performance and monitor program effectiveness.

Student Grouping: The design relies on multi-age groupings. The concept of the "moving diamond," a four-person support network for each student, can also be considered a different type of grouping for students promoting interactions with adults, teachers, and peers.

Curriculum and Instruction: Curriculum combines content areas, skills, and behaviors. Content areas include math, science, geography and history; English-language arts; the arts; health and fitness; and a second language.   Skills and behaviors include effective communication, problem-solving, critical thinking, social cooperation, self-discipline, responsible citizenship, and a life style that values wellness and aesthetics. Curricula for grades 11–12 include job preparation and advanced academic studies. Instruction is expected to reflect current cognitive theories of learning and intelligence, motivations, and individual differences. The designers advocate the following methods: thematic and interdisciplinary instruction, team teaching, and multi-age classrooms. Teachers receive a prototype "tool box" or library of resources, including curricular units and assessments, that they can use as models to develop their own instructional materials.

Professional Development: The professional development plan involves intensive multi-day training institutes (offered during teachers' off-track weeks) and weekly 1–2 hour training sessions. Much of this is collaborative small-group work with clusters of teachers modeling and coaching each other. Teachers have two hours of pupil-free planning time each week (on the same day, permitting collaborative work). Management training will be provided to the site leadership team.

Community Involvement: Each student is provided with mentors or advocates from among older children, parents or community volunteers, and teachers. These advocates form a team called a "moving diamond" to support the child in his or her educational goals. Town meetings provide parents a voice in the school.

Integrated Social Services: The health and social services integration component was rethought over the last year. In its newer version, health and social service integration is thought of as an "enabling" activity linked to changing instruction. Enablers include resource coordination, crisis/emergency assistance and prevention, student and family assistance, community outreach and volunteer recruitment, home involvement with schooling, and classroom-focused enabling. The designers expect that this model will help to (1) increase the capacity of student services by connecting school-based services, e.g., school nurse, attendance and truancy, various psychological services, with community-based agencies providing similar services; and (2) link what is done by social and health service providers with what occurs in the classroom.

Staffing: Not specifically addressed, except that there will be lead teachers. The participation of the teacher's union helps ensure that organization and staffing issues will be addressed in a collaborative fashion.

Technology: A guiding principle is that technology is a tool to be used. Learning centers employ technology for instruction, communication, and data-retrieval purposes. The project includes establishing a "product development" technology center in the school for use by students and the community. Teachers receive notebook computers that they are trained to use as a "creation station" for their tool box products.

MODERN RED SCHOOLHOUSE (MRSH)

Guiding the MRSH design to "break the mold" of American schooling are several principles and assumptions. They include the following:

- six national goals for education;
- all students can learn;
- a common culture that is represented by a core curriculum and SCANS[2] generic competencies;
- principals and teachers with the freedom to organize instruction;
- schools accountable through meaningful assessments;
- use of advanced technology to achieve results; and
- choice in attending a MRSH.

Design Team Leaders: Sally Kilgore and Leslie Lenkowsky.

Governance: The designers require a school plan and school-level autonomy in the areas of budgeting, hiring and staffing, and out-

---

[2]The Secretary's Commission on Achieving Necessary Skills. See U.S. Department of Labor (1992).

sourcing of services. Multiple teams within the school ensure more teacher participation and the participation of those outside the school.

Standards: The design develops its own unique set of world-class standards for all students that reflect high expectations associated with Hirsch's Cultural Literacy[3] curriculum for students in the elementary grades and with SCANS competencies and Advanced Placement tests for students in the intermediate and upper grades.

Assessments: Student performance is measured by various assessments, including tests, watershed assessments, and embedded assessments. Schools are expected to adopt MRSH's standards and assessments.

Student Grouping: Design promotes multi-age, multi-year groupings with few pull-outs. New instructional strategies will promote individualized instruction and multiple regroupings during project work.

Curriculum and Instruction: The design advocates a curriculum founded on Core Knowledge. Core Knowledge will account for about 50 percent of the curricula, allowing leeway for a school's own curricular emphasis. The elementary students make use of Hirsch's Cultural Literacy curriculum, which is sequenced in a year-by-year fashion. During the second year of Phase 2, the design team plans to develop curricular frameworks for intermediate and upper grade students that reflect MRSH world-class standards. The design conceives of teachers reorganizing instruction thematically across grades, integrating across subjects, and making use of computer technology. "Hudson Units" are a means to "capture" curricular units and connect them into a holistic system of standards, assessments, content, resources, and pedagogy. Students' performance on a "collection" of Hudson Units is expected to add up to mastery of MRSH world-class standards. The meaning of Hudson Unit has evolved over the past six months. Teachers develop Hudson units with guidance by the design team.

---

[3]Hirsch (1988).

The design advocates the more flexible use of time so that all students can meet standards. Instruction would be self-paced. Students would be in heterogeneous, multi-aged clusters with the same teacher for several years. Instruction would emphasize methods to promote student problem-solving and thinking. Acknowledging that all students are capable of learning, albeit at different paces, the MRSH design calls for students to engage in self-paced learning and to organize their learning efforts in accordance with an Individual Education Compact negotiated by the student, parents, and teacher.

Professional Development: The designers conceive of a two-part strategy. The first strategy calls for MRSH to train teachers to implement core features of the design. The other strategy is establishment of a self-sustained professional development program designed at the school level. The details of these strategies are not fully developed; they are to be developed by consultants.

Community Involvement: This is not a heavily emphasized element in the design.

Integrated Social Services: Implementing schools are expected to engage social agencies operating locally to assist "at risk" pre-K though grade 12 students. This is a district responsibility, although an expert consultant will facilitate site efforts. The school's primary emphasis will be on education. It is expected that community service agencies will provide their primary emphases.

Staffing: The designers advocate a MRSH teaching force consisting of adults from a wide variety of backgrounds made possible by (1) implementing school autonomy over teacher selection and hiring, and (2) curricular change.

Technology: The designers scaled back technology in response to a budget cut (by NASDC) in late spring 1993. The resulting strategy includes a schoolwide computer network and installation of multi-use microcomputers in classrooms. Teachers will use classroom computers to track students' progress through Hudson Units and Individual Education Compacts. Students will use the computers for instructional and information access purposes.

NATIONAL ALLIANCE FOR RESTRUCTURING EDUCATION (NA)

Instead of promoting change school by school, the National Alliance provides a framework for all levels of the education system (state and local education agencies as well as schools) to support restructuring of schools. The vision is based on the belief that systemic change requires a combination of top-down and bottom-up strategies. The alliance combines member sites and outside experts into a networked umbrella of unifying tasks and goals. The anticipated scope of the effort is to eventually include about 12 percent of the national student population. The design is divided into five "task areas" described below.

Design Team Leaders: Judy Codding and Marc Tucker.

Standards and Assessments: All National Alliance sites are members of the New Standards Project (NSP), a collaboration of the National Center on Education and the Economy, the National Alliance, and the Learning Research and Development Center at the University of Pittsburgh. The effort goes beyond the National Alliance with a total of 20 states signed on to the project. NSP is both developing new standards and incorporating existing high standards in an outcome-based system of assessments.

Alliance sites agree to keep indicators of progress known as Vital Signs to measure whether sites are moving toward the goals of systemic change. Two kinds of measurement are being developed: changes in terms of student performance and indicators of changes in student experiences.

Learning Environments: The design sponsors a number of initiatives aimed at enhancing the curriculum, professional development strategies, and instructional resources to increase learning in schools. The task is an amalgamation of what used to be three separate components of the design: curriculum and instruction, school-to-work focus, and technology as an important part of instruction. The learning environment task is intertwined with the NSP in that learning outcomes provide the starting point from which teachers develop units of study that are shared across the alliance schools. Fundamental to the task is the emphasis on improving the learning environment through professional development opportunities that involve direct interactions among participants and with experts outside the school through a variety of networking devices.

Integrated Social Services: Alliance sites are tasked with developing better ways to integrate health and human services with the schools to serve children's emotional, physical, and academic growth. The task is results-based, keyed to agreed-upon descriptions of what communities and schools want for children, such as students coming to school ready to learn.

High-Performance Management: Alliance sites adapt for education the principles and techniques developed by American business known as high-performance management. These include strategic management, human resources management, Total Quality Management, decentralized decisionmaking and empowerment, and accountability and incentive systems. At the school level, principals are trained in these areas to better support the integration and implementation of the design tasks.

Community Involvement/Public Engagement: Alliance sites at the state, district, and school levels are tasked with developing methods for informing and involving parents and the public in the school and restructuring process.

Evolving Design: The specific activities subsumed under each of these tasks continues to evolve; none are in a finished form. For example, a number of activities this year are designed to develop a school-to-work plan and to begin working on designs for the high school of the future.

ROOTS & WINGS (RW)

The design is intended for elementary schools with fairly large allocations of Title I funds. The Roots component of the design intends to prevent failure. It emphasizes working with children and their families to ensure that children develop the basic skills and habits they need to do well in succeeding years. The Wings component emphasizes a highly motivating curriculum with instructional strategies that encourage children to grow to their full potential and aspire to higher levels of learning. The means to accomplish both components lies in manipulating existing resources in the school, especially Chapter I funds, to provide better instruction.

Design Team Leaders: Robert Slavin and Nancy Madden.

Governance: The design encourages, but does not require, site-based management under a school improvement team, with the principal acting as CEO. The design relies on the ability of the school to control internal allocations of resources, especially federal and state funds, and staff positions. This requires some understanding between the school, district, state, and federal government about the use of funds. The design team has found few legal barriers to the arrangement.

Standards: The design goal is to improve the performance of all students by raising the average performance and reducing the number of low performers. The design relies on Maryland state tests now in development.

Assessments: Assessments will be increasingly performance-based with hands-on demonstrations and portfolios. The strategy is to position Roots and Wings schools to perform increasingly better on assessments evolving as part of a national move toward improved outcomes, rather than to develop a set of assessment tools unique to Roots and Wings.

Student Grouping: Pull-out programs will be eliminated as special teachers, volunteers, and others work in the classroom or after school with students who need additional help. During some parts of the day homogeneous groupings of students will be used for developing specific skills, say, reading skills. Rather than permanent assignment to a group, each student will be assessed and reassigned to new groups as appropriate every eight weeks. The idea is to provide individual attention to those who need it so that they can move from one group to another as they progress. Groupings for math would be different from groupings for reading. During World Lab and other parts of the school day, children will be in heterogeneous groups working in problem-solving modes.

Curriculum and Instruction: The structure of the curriculum will change to encompass three components. First, the schools will use an improved Success for All component for reading and writing skills. The design team is also providing a math component modeled after the reading component and incorporating new standards from the National Council of Teachers of Mathematics (NCTM). Finally, much of the rest of the day will be devoted to an interdisciplinary, hands-on component called World Lab, which integrates science, social studies, math, language arts, and key skills. Instruction will change dramatically. The problem-solving modes and group learning process will require different teacher instructional styles moving away from lecture formats to that of a guide. Learning will become more activity-based.

Professional Development: The role of the RW facilitator after implementation is to provide release time to teachers, assemble materials, observe their instruction and suggest improvements, and model the design elements.

Community Involvement: The family support coordinator is responsible for developing volunteers in the schools, structuring the before-school and after-school programs to address individual needs, making home visits to families with children in need, and in general ensuring that children come to school ready to learn.

Integrated Social Services: The focus of ties to the family and community services is on infants, toddlers, and school-age children. Social services will be coordinated through a site-based team run by a family support coordinator at each school (possible through the reallocation of Title I funds) and facilitated by a district move toward more integrated services.

Staffing: The design includes two new staff positions in the school: the family support coordinator, described above, and a Roots and Wings facilitator to ensure that the design is established and maintained.

Technology: The instruction requires additional computer and other resources to provide students with access to hands-on, instructional software and educational resources. However, computers are not a central piece of the design.

DESCRIPTION OF THE SITES

The characteristics of the first set of sites is important for under-standing the implementation of each of these designs and will be of particular interest to potential adopters of NASDC designs. The fol-lowing paragraphs describe the NASDC sites.

As of spring 1994, the nine design teams have enlisted 138 schools to implement and test the designs. However, the number of schools involved with each design varies considerably (see Table B.1). National Alliance brings the greatest number of sites: 65 schools. Los Angeles Learning Centers and Co-NECT have the fewest, one and two schools, respectively.

Table B.1

Number of Schools, by Design Team

	Elementary	Middle School	Secondary	Other[a]	Total
AC	5	1	2	0	8
AT	7	3	3	0	13
CLC	2	1	0	4	7
CON	1	0	0	1	2
EL	5	2	2	3	12
LALC	0	0	0	1	1
MRSH	18	5	3	0	26
NA	32	12	15	6	65
RW	4	0	0	0	4
Total	74	24	25	15	138

[a]The "Other" category includes K–8 and K–12 schools as well as one 6–10 school.

REPRESENTATIVENESS OF NASDC SCHOOLS

The NASDC designs reflect the array of characteristics seen in the general population of schools but do not exactly match national averages. Indicators for comparisons are geographic setting, grade levels covered, size, and poverty level.[1]

Twenty-nine percent of the schools affiliated with NASDC design teams are located in rural areas. This proportion is comparable to the national figure of 27 percent.[2]

In addition, 54 percent of NASDC schools are at the elementary level, including no grade higher than 6, compared with 50.1 percent nationally.

The average size of elementary schools[3] differs from the national average. The average size of NASDC elementary schools is 534 students and the national average is 458.[4] At the secondary level,[5] the difference is even more significant. The average size of NASDC secondary schools is 933 students and the national average is 678.[6] The range of NASDC school sizes is quite large in both levels. The smallest elementary school has only 50 students and the largest has 1900. Similarly, the smallest secondary school enrolls 69 students and the largest enrolls 2181.

The NASDC design teams have chosen a set of schools with a higher poverty level than the national average. Although the NASDC average for students receiving free lunch is 40 percent, the national average of the percentage of students receiving free or reduced-price lunch is 32 percent.[7]

---

[1] All of the NASDC information presented here is current as of fall 1993.

[2] NCES (1993), p. 70.

[3] Includes schools beginning with grade 6 or below and with no grade higher than 8. Middle schools are categorized as secondary schools. (Definition from NCES, 1993.)

[4] NCES (1993), p. 106.

[5] Includes schools with grades no lower than 7. Middle schools are categorized as secondary schools. (Definition from NCES, 1993.)

[6] NCES (1993), p. 107.

[7] NCES (1993), p. 383.

DESIGN TEAM AVERAGE COMPARED TO NATIONAL AVERAGE

These NASDC averages are skewed by the dominance of the National Alliance (schools involved with the National Alliance account for over half of the NASDC schools). Thus, a more detailed design level view is provided.[8]

Although most of the design teams are implementing their designs in a wide range of settings, three have not chosen any schools located in rural areas: CON, EL, and LALC. In contrast, RW is affiliated with no urban schools, and one small city school. All of the teams have implemented their designs in elementary schools, and three presently are not involved with secondary schools: CON, LALC, and RW.

The average sizes of elementary schools for each design team are close to the national average with three exceptions: Audrey Cohen elementary schools are slightly larger than the national average, and the CON and CLC schools are slightly smaller than the national average. The LALC team, working with a combined elementary/middle school, is the only team that deviates significantly from the national norm. Figure B.1 graphs the average number of students in each design team's elementary schools. The horizontal line indicates the national average.

The range and average size for each design team's elementary schools fall within the expected range, with the exception of CLC schools, which are small, and the LALC school, which is quite large (see Table B.2). All of the design teams cover a wide range of elementary school sizes, except CON and LALC, design teams involved with only two and one schools, respectively.

Greater variations in design team averages are seen in secondary schools than in the average size of elementary schools. The average size of secondary schools of three teams (AT, MRSH, and NA) is more than 200 students above the national average. The average size of schools involved with CLC and EL is more than 200 students below

---

[8]The data for the MRSH schools in Charlotte were unavailable at the time of this report.

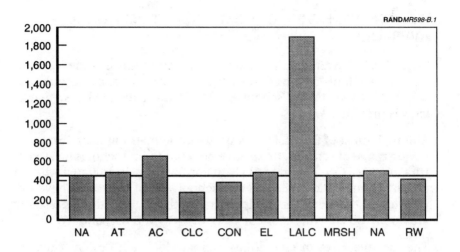

Figure B.1—Average Size of Elementary Schools, by Design Team

Table B.2

Number, Range, and Average Size of Participating Elementary Schools, by Design Team

	Number	Minimum	Maximum	Average
AT	7	146	749	479
AC	5	375	954	650
CON	2	348	420	384
CLC	3	92	635	280
EL	7	337	922	483
LALC	1	1900	1900	1900
MRSH	18	293	543	458
NA	36	175	942	505
RW	4	276	622	423

the national average. It should be noted that the CLC figure represents only one middle school. Figure B.2 graphs the average size of each team's secondary schools. The horizontal line represents the national average. CON, LALC, and RW have been excluded from this graph because they are affiliated only with elementary schools.

Table B.3 shows the range and average size for each design team's secondary schools.

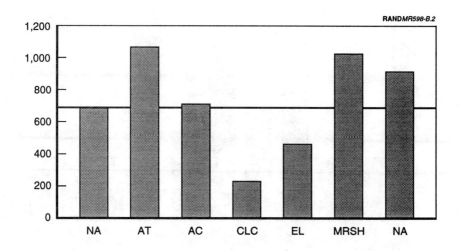

Figure B.2—Average Size of Secondary Schools, by Design Team

Table B.3

Number, Range, and Average Size of Participating Secondary Schools, by
Design Team

	Number	Minimum	Maximum	Average
AT	6	297	2181	1067
AC	3	589	950	713
CON	0	0	—	0
CLC	1	235	235	235
EL	5	168	576	460
LALC	0	0	0	0
MRSH	5	505	1361	1020
NA	27	69	2100	912
RW	0	0	0	0

Most of the design teams are involved with schools with a higher poverty rate than the national average. Only one design team's school averages fall well below the national average: MRSH. The average percentage of students receiving free lunch in the schools affiliated with LALC, CON, and AC are at least 100 percent higher than the national average. Figure B.3 graphs the average percentage of

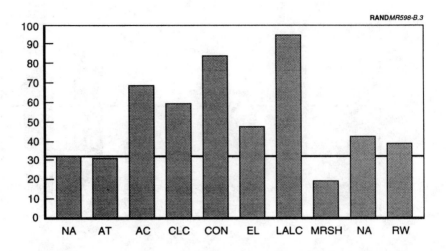

Figure B.3—Average Percentage of Students Receiving Free or Reduced-
Price School Lunch, by Design Team

students receiving free lunch in each of design team's schools.[9]
Again, the horizontal line indicates the national average.

SUMMARY

In general, then, the teams chose a set of schools representative of a
cross-section of the nation's schools. The implementing schools represent the range of settings, sizes, and socioeconomic status with two
exceptions. The average size of both CLC's elementary and secondary schools is lower than the national average. This is because of
the nature of the CLC design—the team is working with several charter schools, which are in their first year of implementation and are
expected to be small.

---

[9]The figures for CLC and RW represent combined totals for students receiving free and
reduced-price lunch and are therefore slightly inflated.

Berman, Paul, and Milbrey McLaughlin, *Federal Programs Supporting Educational Change, the Findings in Review*, Santa Monica, Calif.: RAND, R-1589/4-HEW, 1975.

Bimber, Bruce, *The Decentralization Mirage, Comparing Decisionmaking Arrangements in Four High Schools*, Santa Monica, Calif.: RAND, MR-459-GGF/LE, 1994.

Bodilly, Susan, et al., *Integrating Academic and Vocational Education: Lessons from Eight Early Innovators*, Santa Monica, Calif.: RAND, R-4265-NCRVE/UCB, 1993.

Bodilly, Susan, Susanna Purnell, and Paul Hill, *A Formative Assessment of the General Electric Foundation's College Bound Program*, Santa Monica, Calif.: RAND, MR-463-GEF, 1994.

Goodlad, John, *A Place Called School*, New York: McGraw-Hill Book Company, 1984.

Gross, Neal, Joseph Giaquinta, and Marilyn Bernstein, *Implementing Organizational Innovations*, New York: Basic Books, 1971.

Hirsch, E. D., Jr., *Cultural Literacy*, New York: Vintage Books, 1988.

Liberman, Ann, et al., *Early Lessons in Restructuring Schools*, National Center for Restructuring Education, Schools, and Teaching (NCREST), New York: Teachers College, Columbia University, August 1991.

Mazmanian, Daniel, and Paul Sabatier, *Effective Policy Implementation*, Lexington, Massachusetts: Lexington Books, 1981.

McLaughlin, Milbrey, "The RAND Change Agent Study Revisited: Macro Perspectives and Micro Realities," *Education Researcher*, December 1990, pp. 11–16.

Mirel, Jeffrey, "School Reform Unplugged: The Bensenville New American School Project, 1991–93," *American Educational Research Journal*, Vol. 31, No. 3, Fall 1994, pp. 481–518.

National Center for Education Statistics (NCES), *Digest of Education Statistics 1993*, U.S. Department of Education, Office of Education Research and Improvement, NCES 93-292.

New American Schools Development Corporation (NASDC), *Designs for a New Generation of American Schools, A Request for Proposals*, Arlington, Virginia, October 1991.

Policy Studies Associates, Inc., *School Reform for Youth at Risk: An Analysis of Six Change Models, Vol. I. Summary Analysis*, U.S. Department of Education, 1994.

Rivlin, Alice P., and Michael Timpane, *Planned Variation in Education*, Washington, D.C.: Brookings Institution, 1975.

U.S. Department of Labor, *SCANS, Learning a Living: A Blueprint for High Performance*, April 1992.